# MEXICAN
and Latin American
Phrase Book

# MEXICAN
## and Latin American
## Phrase Book

PANORAMA EDITORIAL, S.A.

# Contents

# Introduction

The Mexican and Latin American Phrase Book is designed to help the reader who has no previous knowledge of the language. With its aid he should be able to make himself readily understood on all occasions and to cope with the host of minor problems —and some major ones— that can arise when on holiday or travelling in **Mexico**.

The key to successful speech in a foreign language is pronunciation, and an outline of the principles of vowel and consonant sounds and their usage in Spanish is to be found at the beginning of this book. This is followed by a section dealing with the essential elements of Spanish grammar. A close study of these two sections and constant reference to them will be of the utmost value: with the pattern of sentence construction in mind and a feeling for the sound of the language, the reader will be well equipped to use the phrases in this book.

These are set out in logical order, beginning with the various means of travel and entry into the country. The section on accommodations has been thoroughly reviewed. Particular attention is paid in the chapter on food and drink to the specialty dishes from the different regions and in the section on sport, there is a chapter describing the principles of the bullfight. Shopping, too, is covered in detail. The reader will find a selection of appropriate phrases, easy to refer to and simple to use, when he wishes to acquire an article of Mexican handicraft that will be a constant reminder of his sojourn south of the border.

Entertainment, sightseeing, public services, and general conversations in the hotel bar are all covered, and there is an important section of commercial and banking phrases of particular value to the businessman. In addition to carefully chosen phrases, each section includes an appropriate vocabulary which is as comprehensive as possible, and at the end of the book there are quick-reference metric conversion tables for the more important temperatures, weights and measures.

The **Mexican** and **Latin American** Phrase Book will not only enable the traveller to handle any situation with confidence but will help to make his stay in **Mexico** and **Latin America** a more enjoyable one.

# Guide to Spanish Pronunciation

This is intended for people with no previous knowledge of Spanish and is based on English pronunciation. This means that it is not entirely accurate but the reader who pays careful attention to this section should, with practice, be able to make himself understood reasonably well in Spanish.

## The Vowels

| LETTER | APPROXIMATE PRONUNCIATION | EXAMPLE |
|---|---|---|
| a | like *a* in father | **patata** |
| e | like *a* in mate | **mesa** |
| i | 1. like *ee* in meet | **chico** |
| | 2. before another vowel like the *y* in yet | **tienda** |
| o | like *o* in go, toe | **todo** |
| u | 1. like *oo* in shoot | **mucho** |
| | 2. before another vowel like the *w* in wet | **bueno** |
| y | only pronounced as a vowel when alone or at the end of a word, like *ee* in bee | **y, rey** |

# Pronunciation

## The Consonants

| LETTER | APPROXIMATE PRONUNCIATION | EXAMPLE |
|---|---|---|
| d f k l m n p t y | pronounced as in English | |
| c | 1. before *e* and *i* like the s in sick | centro cinco |
| | 2. elsewhere like *k* in kid | poco |
| ch | like *ch* in church | muchacho |
| g | 1. before *e* and *i* like the *h* in hot | gente surgir |
| | 2. elsewhere like *g* in go | gato |
| h | always silent in Spanish | haber |
| j | like the *h* in hold | bajo |
| ll | like *lli* in million | llamar |
| ñ | like *ni* in onion | señor |
| qu | like *k* in kind | que |
| r | slightly trilled like the Scottish *r* | rey |
| rr | strongly trilled | perro |
| s | always like *s* in set; never hard like in rose | siempre casa |
| v | 1. usually like *b* in boy | vaso |
| | 2. between two vowels, as an intermediate sound between *b* and *v* | ave |
| z | like the *s* in said | manzana |

## Stress

Words ending in a vowel are stressed on the next to last syllable: **chico, mañana.**

Words ending in a consonant, except for *n* or *s*, are stressed on the last syllable: **señor, ciudad, hablar.**

Exceptions to these rules have an accent written on the stressed syllable: **aquí, lección, difícil.**

# A Little Grammar in Action

## Nouns

All nouns in Spanish are either masculine or feminine whether they refer to living beings or inanimate objects.

Nouns ending in -*o* are masculine and those ending in -*a* are usually feminine. Nouns ending in a consonant or -*e* may be either masculine or feminine.

**el chico** the boy
**el hombre** the man
**la madre** the mother
**la casa** the house
**la mujer** the woman

To form the plural nouns ending in a vowel add -*s* and those ending in a consonant add -*es*. The word for 'the' is **los** before masculine and **las** before feminine nouns.

**los chicos** the boys
**las mujeres** the women

The word for 'a' (or indefinite article) is **un** before a masculine noun and **una** before a feminine noun.

**un tren** a train
**una casa** a house

The word 'of' showing possession is translated by **de** in Spanish, **de** and **el** being shortened to **del**.

**el libro del chico** the boy's book
**la madre de la mujer** the woman's mother
**las puertas de las casas** the doors of the houses

4

# Adjectives

Adjectives agree in number and gender with the noun they accompany; that is, they change their endings according to whether the noun is masculine, feminine or plural. They generally follow the noun. Adjectives ending in -*o* change to -*a* in the feminine.

**el chico pequeño** the little boy
**la casa roja** the red house

Adjectives ending in -*e* and most of those ending in a consonant do not change in the feminine.

**el libro azul** the blue book
**la puerta azul** the blue door
**un hombre inteligente** a clever man
**una mujer inteligente** a clever woman

To form the plural adjectives ending in -*o*, -*a*, or -*e* add -*s*; adjectives ending in a consonant add -*es*.

**las chicas bonitas** the pretty girls
**los libros azules** the blue books

To form the comparative and superlative forms put **más** before the adjective.

**un libro caro** an expensive book
**un libro más caro** a more expensive book
**el libro más caro** the most expensive book

## Demonstrative Adjectives

The words for 'this' and 'that' are as follows.

**este hombre** this mán
**estos hombres** these men

5

# Grammar

**esta mujer** this woman
**estas mujeres** these women

**aquel libro** that book
**aquellos libros** those books

**aquella casa** that house
**aquellas casas** those houses

## Possessive Adjectives

The words for 'my', 'your', 'his', etc., change their form
according to whether the noun they refer to is masculine,
feminine or plural.

|  | SINGULAR | PLURAL |
|---|---|---|
| my | mi | mis |
| your | tu | tus |
| his/her/its | su | sus |
| our | nuestro(a) | nuestros(as) |
| your | vuestro(a) | vuestros(as) |
| their | su | sus |

**mi hijo** my son
**mis padres** my parents

**tu hermana** your sister
**tus amigos** your friends

**su madre** his/her mother
**sus libros** his/her books

**nuestro coche** our car
**nuestras cartas** our letters

**vuestra casa** your house
**vuestros lápices** your pencils

**su maleta** their suitcase
**sus cuartos** their rooms

## Personal Pronouns

The words for 'I', 'you', 'he', etc., are as follows.

1. When used as the subject of a verb:

| | |
|---|---|
| yo canto | I sing |
| tu cantas | you sing |
| usted canta | you sing (polite form) |
| él canta | he sings |
| nosotros(as) cantamos | we sing |
| vosotros(as) cantáis | you sing |
| ustedes cantan | you sing (polite form) |
| ellos(as) cantan | they sing |

2. When used as the direct object of a verb:

| | |
|---|---|
| **Señor López me conoce.** | Mr. López knows me. |
| te | you |
| le (polite form) | you (masc.) |
| la (polite form) | you (fem.) |
| le/lo | him |
| la | her |
| nos | us |
| os | you |
| los (polite form) | you (masc. pl.) |
| las (polite form) | you (fem. pl.) |
| los/les | them (masc.) |
| las | them (fem.) |

**Note.** The second person plural forms (vuestro, vosotros, os) are rarely used in Mexico, the polite forms (usted ed.) being used instead.

# Grammar

3. When used as the indirect object of a verb:

| Señor López me dice | | Mr. López says to me |
|---|---|---|
| | te | you |
| | le (polite form) | you |
| | le | him/her |
| | nos | us |
| | os | you |
| | les (polite form) | you |
| | les | them |

When used as the direct or indirect object pronouns are placed in front of the verb. When two pronouns in the third person occur together the indirect pronoun **le** or **les** is replaced by **se**.

**Señor López se lo dice**   Mr. López tells (it) to him

4. When used after a preposition:

| Estos libros son para mí | These books are for me |
|---|---|
| ti | you |
| usted (polite form) | you |
| él/ella | him/her |
| nosotros(as) | us |
| vosotros(as) | you |
| ustedes (polite form) | you (plural) |
| ellos | them (masc.) |
| ellas | them (fem.) |

In Spanish, the polite way of addressing people is to use **usted** (often abbreviated to **Vd.**) and **le** when talking to one person and **ustedes** (often abbreviated to **Vds.**) and **les** when talking to more than one person. **Tu**, etc., and its plural **vosotros** are the familiar forms and should be used only when talking to children, relatives and close friends.

## Verbs

The whole subject of Spanish verbs is too complicated for detailed discussion in a phrase book but for the traveller who wants a quick grasp of verbs with which he can communicate while staying in a Spanish-speaking country, the following basic rules would be helpful.

### Regular Verbs

Most Spanish verbs are regular in their formation and fall into one of three categories or conjugations. Note that the subject pronouns are usually omitted (except for the polite forms **usted** and **ustedes**) since the verb endings show which person is referred to.

1. Verbs ending in -ar in the infinitive.

| | |
|---|---|
| **comprar** | to buy |
| **yo compro** | I buy |
| **tu compras** | you buy |
| **usted compra** | you buy |
| **él/ella compra** | he/she buys |
| **nosotros compramos** | we buy |
| **vosotros compráis** | you buy |
| **ustedes compran** | you buy |
| **ellos/ellas compran** | they buy (m., f.) |

2. Verbs ending in -er in the infinitive.

| | |
|---|---|
| **vender** | to sell |
| **yo vendo** | I sell |
| **tu vendes** | you sell |
| **usted vende** | you sell |
| **él/ella vende** | he/she sells |
| **nosotros vendemos** | we sell |
| **vosotros vendéis** | you sell |
| **ustedes venden** | you sell |
| **ellos/ellas venden** | they sell (m., f.) |

# Grammar

3. Verbs ending in -ir in the infinitive.

| vivir | to live |
|---|---|
| yo vivo | I live |
| tu vives | you live |
| usted vive | you live |
| él/ella vive | he/she lives |
| nosotros vivimos | we live |
| vosotros vivís | you live |
| ustedes viven | you live |
| ellos/ellas viven | they (m., f.) live |

To form the negative of a verb **no** is placed before it:

**No vendemos libros** we don't sell books

## Irregular Verbs

The following are a few of the more useful common irregular verbs.

| ser | to be | estar | to be |
|---|---|---|---|
| yo soy | I am | yo estoy | I am |
| tu eres | you are | tu estás | you are |
| usted es | you are | usted está | you are |
| él/ella es | he/she is | él/ella está | he/she is |
| nosotros somos | we are | nosotros estamos | we are |
| vosotros sois | you are | vosotros estáis | you are |
| ustedes son | you are | ustedes están | you are |
| ellos/ellas son | they are | ellos/ellas están | they are |

To be' is translated by **ser** when it describes a permanent condition. It is translated by **estar** when it indicates a temporary state or location.

**el hielo es frío** ice is cold
**es español** he is Spanish
**estamos en Texas** we are in Texas

| haber | to have | tener | to have (possessive) |
|---|---|---|---|
| **yo he** | I have | **yo tengo** | I have |
| **tu has** | you have | **tu tienes** | you have |
| **usted ha** | you have | **usted tiene** | you have |
| **él/ella ha** | he/she has | **él/ella tiene** | he/she has |
| **nosotros habemos** | we have | **nosotros tenemos** | we have |
| **vosotros habéis** | you have | **vosotros tenéis** | you have |
| **ustedes han** | you have | **ustedes tienen** | you have |
| **ellos(as) han** | they have | **ellos(as) tienen** | they have |

**haber** is used only to form the compound tenses of verbs:

**he comprado un lápiz** I have bought a pencil

**tener** is used in all the other meanings of 'have'.

**tengo un lápiz** I have a pencil

| dar | to give | decir | to say |
|---|---|---|---|
| **yo doy** | I give | **yo digo** | I say |
| **tu das** | you give | **tu dices** | you say |
| **usted da** | you give | **usted dice** | you say |
| **él/ella da** | he/she gives | **él/ella dice** | he/she says |
| **nosotros damos** | we give | **nosotros decimos** | we say |
| **vosotros dáis** | you give | **vosotros decís** | you say |
| **ustedes dan** | you give | **ustedes dicen** | you say |
| **ellos(as) dan** | they give | **ellos(as) dicen** | they say |

| hacer | to make, do | ir | to go |
|---|---|---|---|
| **yo hago** | I make | **yo voy** | I go |
| **tu haces** | you make | **tu vas** | you go |
| **usted hace** | you make | **usted va** | you go |
| **él/ella hace** | he/she makes | **él/ella va** | he/she goes |
| **nosotros hacemos** | we make | **nosotros vamos** | we go |
| **vosotros hacéis** | you make | **vosotros váis** | you go |
| **ustedes hacen** | you make | **ustedes van** | you go |
| **ellos(as) hacen** | they make | **ellos(as) van** | they go |

11

# Grammar

| | | | |
|---|---|---|---|
| poder | to be able, can | poner | to put |
| yo puedo | I can | yo pongo | I put |
| tu puedes | you can | tu pones | you put |
| usted puede | you can | usted pone | you put |
| él/ella puede | he/she can | él/ella pone | he/she puts |
| nosotros podemos | we can | nosotros ponemos | we put |
| vosotros podéis | you can | vosotros ponéis | you put |
| ustedes pueden | you can | ustedes ponen | you put |
| ellos(as) pueden | they can | ellos(as) ponen | they put |
| | | | |
| querer | to want | traer | to bring |
| yo quiero | I want | yo traigo | I bring |
| tu quieres | you want | tu traes | you bring |
| usted quiere | you want | usted trae | you bring |
| él/ella quiere | he/she wants | él/ella trae | he/she brings |
| nosotros queremos | we want | nosotros traemos | we bring |
| vosotros queréis | you want | vosotros traéis | you bring |
| ustedes quieren | you want | ustedes traen | you bring |
| ellos(as) quieren | they want | ellos(as) traen | they bring |
| | | | |
| venir | to come | ver | to see |
| yo vengo | I come | yo veo | I see |
| tu vienes | you come | tu ves | you see |
| usted viene | you come | usted ve | you see |
| él/ella viene | he/she comes | él/ella ve | he/she sees |
| nosotros venimos | we come | nosotros vemos | we see |
| vosotros venís | you come | vosotros véis | you see |
| ellos(as) vienen | they come | ellos(as) ven | they see |

# Spoken Spanish

The Spanish-speaking world is, indeed extensive comprising not only Spain and the Balearic and Canary Islands, but the whole of the Latin American continent as well, excepting Brazil. Perhaps surprisingly to those unacquainted with the history of Imperial Spain, it reaches as far as the Philippines.

## Mexico

The regions of Mexico which are of greatest interest to the visitor include not only its capital city or the impeccable white sand beaches of Cancun, Puerto Vallarta, Ixtapa-Zihuatanejo, etc., but also some of the old colonial towns which are located inland. The following is a brief list of some of the places the tourist will find of interest.

**MEXICO CITY.** Situated in the heart of the Federal District at an altitude of 7349 feet in the Anahuac Valley and surrounded by mountains on all sides. It was founded by the Aztecs, conquered by the Spaniards, ruled over as an Empire by Maximilian and finally converted into a Republic. The city has a varied and romantic history. Today it is one of the world's most vital areas and, as is said of Rome, all roads lead to it. Here the tourist may find a limitless number of attractions such as the beautiful National Museum of Anthropology, University City, the Fine Arts Palace where the Folk Ballet is performed, the venerated Shrine of Guadalupe and in the main square, or 'Zócalo', the National Palace and Metropolitan Cathedral. Here, too, the visitor may witness history being uncovered each Saturday at the archaeological excavations on Guatemala and Republica de Argentina streets. The capital's many attractions include some of the finest restaurants and night clubs in the world. Sports arenas abound, as well as bullfight rings. Here, too, are found all of the charming handicrafts produced throughout the country. A day at San Juan market is a must. And a visit to the Republic of Mexico is unthinkable without including a visit to its very heart.

**GUANAJUATO** is traditionally famous for its silver mining. During the colonial era, it was the richest silver-producing area in the world although it has waned in importance. Situated in the central portion of the country called the 'Bajío', agriculturally it is known as the 'bread basket' of **Mexico**. Its capital city, also called Guanajuato, is famous for its fine examples of Spanish colonial architecture. Nearby San Miguel de Allende has an Art Institute that draws many American and Canadian painters.

**GUERRERO** state is where **ACAPULCO** is situated which, ich as a world famous jet set resort hardly needs an introduction. Modern hotels, discos, restaurants abound. In the same state is to be found the charming old silver mining town of **TAXCO** with its colonial cathedral and silver shops. Nearby one may visit the caves of **CACAHUAMILPA** with their endless stalactite and stalagmite formations ever creating imaginary figures in the eye of the visitor.

**GUADALAJARA,** the capital of **JALISCO** state, is a colonial provincial city surrounded by some of the richest cattle and agricultural areas. This industrial center produces textiles and ceramics. Especially famous are those of Tlalquepaque. Nearby resorts are lakeside **CHAPALA** and **PUERTO VALLARTA** on the Pacific coast. This area contains a quite large American population.

**MICHOACAN** on the Pacific coast is a state of dense forests, lakes and waterfalls amidst volcanic wilds. Agriculture flourishes. Fruits, cereals and coffee have given it the title of 'garden state'. It is famous for its native crafts... lacquerware, sarapes, rebozos. **Morelia** is a delightful colonial town where the hero of the struggle for Independence —**José María Morelos**— was born. It is surrounded by charming villages such as **Tzintzuntzan** and **Quiroga** where many handicraft varieties may be acquired. Close by is **Santa Clara del Cobre** for hand-hammered copper ware. Here, too, is situated **Pátzcuaro** on the lake of the same name which is famous for its delicate white fish. . . blanco de **Pátzcuaro**.

**MORELOS**, just south of the Federal District has as its capital city **CUERNAVACA**, famous for its luxuriant gardens and caressing, balmy climate. . . often called the 'land of eternal spring'. It is a mere 40 minutes by highway from Mexico City and therefore has always been a mecca for tourists as well as a tropical paradise for **Mexico City** residents. Many 'retirees', most importantly Americans, call **Cuernavaca** their home. Close by are **Cuautla** (mineral baths), **Tepoztlán** (rugged scenery) and Lake **Tequesquitengo** (water-skiing and boating).

**OAXACA** in the **Zapoteca-Mixteca** zone of southern **México** has an extensive agricultural production. Of major importance is the pineapple industry. The hot lowlands produce coffee, sugar cane, cacao, vanilla, tropical fruits and hardwoods. Cattle thrive in the luscious green pastureland. **Oaxaca**, the capital of the state, has many interesting tourist attractions including the old **Santo Domingo** cathedral. Nearby are the ruins of **Monte Albán** and **Mitla** with their famous pyramids. **Oaxaca** produces some of the most beautiful handicrafts in the country.

**PUEBLA**, situated two hours by car from the capital is, famous for many things, such as its talavera tiles and ceramics and, of course, **'mole poblano'**. Its most spectacular attribute are the four mighty mountains surrounding it. . . **Ixtaccíhuatl** and **Popocatépetl** on the western border, **La Malinche** in the center and on the eastern fringe, the highest mountain in the country. . . the **Pico de Orizaba**. **Puebla** today is becoming an industrial center of renown which gives a modern aspect to its Spanish provincial appearance.

# Spoken Spanish

**YUCATAN,** far to the southeast, has become an important tourist center with the newly opened Cancun resort having some of the world's most beautiful virgin white sand beaches. Here too are **Cozumel** and **Isla de Mujeres,** both resort islands. The capital of the state, **MERIDA,** is known as the 'white city' and has many points of interest for the tourist. Nearby are the ruins at **Chichén Itzá** and **Uxmal,** capitals of the ancient Mayan civilizations.

Wherever you travel in these regions you will find that a few words spoken in Spanish will help to establish a friendly atmosphere. Here are some simple phrases of greeting and leave-taking:

| | |
|---|---|
| Good morning. | **Buenos días.** |
| Good afternoon. | **Buenas tardes.** |
| Good evening. | **Buenas tardes/noches.** |
| Good night. | **Buenas noches.** |
| How are you? | **¿Cómo está usted?** |
| I'm pleased to meet you. | **Tanto gusto.** |
| How do you do? | **Encantado de conocerle.** |
| Goodbye. | **Adiós.** |

Some words of courtesy. . .

| | |
|---|---|
| Please. | **Por favor.** |
| Thank you. | **Gracias.** |
| It's very kind of you. | **Es usted muy amable.** |
| You are welcome. | **De nada.** |
| Not at all. | **No hay de qué.** |

And some questions. . .

| | |
|---|---|
| Where is the hotel? | **¿Dónde está el hotel?** |
| What did you say? | **¿Qué dijo?** |

| When does the train leave? | ¿Cuándo sale el tren? |
| Who are you? | ¿Quién es usted? |
| How much does it cost? | ¿Cuánto cuesta? |
| Which is the road to. . .? | ¿Cuál es la carretera a. . .? |
| Why are we waiting? | ¿Por qué estamos esperando? |

And finally, some useful common phrases. . .

| Yes. | Sí. |
| No. | No. |
| Why? | ¿Por qué? |
| How? | ¿Cómo? |
| When? | ¿Cuándo? |
| What? | ¿Qué? |
| Where? | ¿Dónde? |
| How much? | ¿Cuánto? |
| How many? | ¿Cuántos? |
| Please speak slowly. | Hable despacio por favor. |
| I do not understand Spanish very well. | No entiendo muy bien el español |
| Will you write it down please? | ¿Lo puede escribir por favor? |
| How do I say. . .? | ¿Cómo se dice. . .? |
| What is the meaning of. . .? | ¿Qué significa. . .? |
| Please show me how this works. | Enséñeme cómo funciona por favor. |
| How far is it to. . .? | ¿Cuál es la distancia a. . .? |
| Where is the nearest. . .? | ¿Cuál es el próximo. . .? |
| What time is it? | ¿Qué hora es? |

17

| | |
|---|---|
| Will you please help me? | ¿Me puede ayudar por favor? |
| Can you point to where we are on this map? | ¿Me puede señalar dónde estamos en este mapa? |
| Which way do I go? | ¿Cómo voy? |
| Is there an official tourist office here? | ¿Hay aquí una Oficina de Turismo? |
| Where is the station/bus terminal/bus stop? | ¿Dónde está la estación terminal de autobús/ parada de autobús? |
| Where do I buy a ticket? | ¿Dónde puedo comprar un boleto? |
| Am I too early? | ¿He llegado demasiado temprano? |
| It is too late. | Es demasiado tarde. |
| We have missed the plane. | Hemos perdido el avión. |
| Do I turn right/left? | ¿Doy vuelta a la derecha/ izquierda? |
| Do I go straight ahead? | ¿Voy todo derecho? |
| What is the name of this street? | ¿Cómo se llama esta calle? |
| How do I get to. . .? | ¿Cómo voy a. . .? |
| How much does it cost? | ¿Cuánto cuesta? |
| It is too expensive. | Es demasiado caro. |
| Please give me the change. | Déme el cambio, por favor. |
| I am tired. | Estoy cansado. |
| I am hungry/thirsty. | Tengo hambre/sed. |
| It is very hot/cold. | Hace mucho calor/ frío. |

| | |
|---|---|
| Please take me to my hotel. | ¿Me lleva al hotel por favor? |
| Is the service included? | ¿Está incluido el servicio? |
| Thank you very much. | Muchas gracias. |

And some idiomatic expressions. . .

| | |
|---|---|
| Go away. | Váyase. |
| Leave me alone. | Déjeme en paz. |
| Shut up. | Cállese. |
| How goes it? | ¿Como va? |
| So so. | Así así. |
| You're joking. | Está usted bromeando. |
| Don't move. | No se mueva. |
| That's it. | Eso es. |
| You're right. | Tiene usted razón. |
| Carry on. | Prosiga. |

# All Aboard

Journeys through Mexico are preferable by car or bus. Air service is the quickest way to get about and national airlines provide excellent service. Travel by train is mostly undertaken by residents rather than by foreigners.

The main highways are well cared for and there are several super highways. Gasoline stations are not overly abundant, therefore the gasoline level should not be allowed to fall too low. If you have time, travel slowly; this is how you reach the heart of the country and where a halting conversation can create a warmth of communication that remains a long time in the memory.

## Arrivals and Departures

### Going through Passport Control and Customs

At most of the main ports of entry there will be someone with a smattering of English, but this is not always the case. It is useful, therefore, to know one or two basic phrases. Apart from making communication easier, they assist in establishing a friendly relationship with officials and often smooth the passage through frontiers.

| | |
|---|---|
| Good morning/afternoon/evening. | **Buenos días/tardes/noches.** |
| Here is my passport. | **Aquí está mi pasaporte.** |
| I am on holiday/on business. | **Estoy de vacaciones/de negocios.** |
| I am visiting relatives/friends. | **Estoy visitando a la familia/los amigos.** |
| Here is my vaccination certificate. | **Aquí está mi certificado de vacunación.** |

20

| | |
|---|---|
| The visa is stamped on page X. | El visado está sellado en la página X. |
| They did not stamp my passport at the entry port. | No sellaron mi pasaporte en la oficina de inmigración. |
| Will you please stamp my passport? It will be a souvenir of my holiday. | ¿Me sella el pasaporte por favor? Será un recuerdo de mis vacaciones. |
| I will stay a few days/two weeks/a month. | Permaneceré unos días/dos semanas/un mes. |
| I am in transit. | Estoy de paso. |
| My wife and I have a joint passport. | Mi mujer y yo tenemos un pasaporte común. |
| The children are on my wife's passport. | Los niños están en el pasaporte de mi esposa. |
| I didn't realise it had expired. | No me dí cuenta de que había caducado. |
| Can I telephone the American consulate? | ¿Puedo llamar al consulado norteamericano? |
| I have nothing to declare. | No tengo nada que declarar. |
| Do you want me to open my suitcases? Which one? | ¿Quiere que abra mis maletas? ¿Cuál? |
| They are all personal belongings. | Todos son efectos personales. |
| I have a few small gifts for my friends. | Traigo unos pequeños regalos para mis amigos. |
| I have 200 cigarettes and a bottle of whiskey. | Tengo doscientos cigarrillos y una botella de licor. |
| They are for my personal consumption. | Son para mi uso personal. |
| Do I have to pay duty? | ¿Tengo que pagar derechos de aduana? |

## Arrivals and Departures

| | |
|---|---|
| I have no other luggage. | **No tengo más equipaje.** |
| Do you want to see my purse/briefcase? | **¿Quiere ver mi bolso/ portafolio?** |
| I can't find my keys. | **No puedo encontrar mis llaves.** |
| I have 2000 pesos in currency and a hundred dollars in travellers' checks. | **Tengo dos mil pesos en efectivo y cien dólares en cheques de viajero.** |
| I can't afford to pay duty. | **No puedo pagar los derechos de aduana.** |
| Can you keep it in bond? | **¿Puede guardarlo como depósito bajo fianza?** |
| Here is a list of the souvenirs I have bought. | **Aquí tiene una lista de los regalos que he comprado.** |
| You haven't marked my suitcase. | **No ha marcado mi maleta.** |
| May I leave now? | **¿Me puedo ir ahora?** |

## At Airports, Terminals and Stations

| | |
|---|---|
| Where can I find a porter? | ¿Dónde puedo encontrar un maletero? |
| a luggage cart? | una carretilla de equipaje? |
| luggage claim section? | entrega de equipaje? |
| Have you seen the representative of my travel agency? | ¿Ha visto al representante de mi compañía de viajes? |
| Take my bag to the bus, taxi, car. | Lleve mi maleta al autobús, taxi, coche. |
| How much per suitcase? | ¿Cuánto por maleta? |

### Toilets

| | |
|---|---|
| Where is the ladies'/men's room? | ¿Dónde está el lavabo de señoras/caballeros? |
| Have you any soap? | ¿Tiene jabón? |
| toilet paper? | papel higiénico? |
| a clean towel? | una toalla limpia? |
| a comb or hair brush? | un peine o cepillo de pelo? |
| Shall I leave a tip? | ¿Dejo propina? |

### Telephone

| | |
|---|---|
| Where are the public telephones? | ¿Dónde están los teléfonos públicos? |
| I need a telephone directory | Necesito un directorio telefónico. |
| Where can I get some change? | ¿Dónde puedo obtener cambio? |

23

## Airports, Terminals and Stations

| | |
|---|---|
| Can I dial this number or do I ask the operator? | ¿Puedo marcar este número o se lo pido a la telefonista? |
| Hello. | ¿Bueno? ¡Bueno! |
| You need a coin. | Necesita una moneda. |
| May I have 557-13-27? | ¿Me da el cinco cincuenta y siete, trece, veintisiete? |
| Can I call collect reverse the charges? | ¿Puedo llamar por cobrar? |
| I want a person-to-person call. | Quiero una llamada personal. |
| I have been cut off. | Me han desconectado. |
| You gave me the wrong number. | Me dio el número equivocado. |
| Is she not in? | ¿No está? |
| Tell her I called. | Dígale que he llamado. |
| My name is. . . | Me llamo. . . |

## Taxi Stand

| | |
|---|---|
| Where can I get a taxi? | ¿Dónde puedo tomar un taxi? |
| Please get me a taxi. | Por favor llame un taxi. |
| Take me to this address. | Lléveme a esta dirección. |
| How much will it cost? | ¿Cuánto costará? |
| That's too much. | Es demasiado. |
| Turn right/left at the next corner. | De vuelta a la derecha/ izquierda en la próxima esquina. |
| Go straight on. | Vaya todo derecho. |
| I'll tell you when to stop. | Yo le diré cuando tiene que parar. |
| Stop. | Pare. |

| I'm in a hurry. | Llevo prisa. |
| Take it easy. | Vaya despacio. |
| Can you please carry my bags? | ¿Puede llevar mis maletas por favor? |

## Signs

| Ticket Office | Despacho de Boletos |
| Car Rentals | Auto-Renta |
| Bus Station | Estación de autobuses (camiones) |
| Escalator | Escalera eléctrica |
| Exit | Salida |
| Information Office | Oficina de Información (Informes) |
| Baggage Counter | Equipaje |
| Platform | Andén |
| Porters | Maleteros |
| Toilet (Men/Women) | Baño (Damas/Caballeros) |
| Subway | Metro |
| Waiting Room | Sala de espera |
| Bus Stop | Parada de autobús |

## Newspaper Stand

| Do you have an American newspaper or magazine? | ¿Tiene un periódico o una revista americana? |
| Which is the local paper? | ¿Cuál es el periódico local? |
| Do you have (train) timetables? | ¿Tiene horarios (de trenes)? |

## Airports, Terminals and Stations

| | |
|---|---|
| Do you have a guide/map of the city? | ¿Tiene una guía/un mapa de la ciudad? |
| Have you any writing paper and envelopes? | ¿Tiene papel de escribir y sobres? |
| a ball point pen? | una pluma? |
| some string? | cuerda? |
| scotch tape? | cinta adhesiva? |
| matches? | cerillos? |
| stamps? | timbres? |

## Information Bureau

| | |
|---|---|
| Is there an information bureau here? | ¿Hay aquí una oficina de información? |
| Have you any brochures? | ¿Tiene algún folleto? |
| Have you a guide to the hotels? | ¿Tiene una guía sobre los hoteles? |
| pensions? | pensiones? |
| youth hostels? | los albergues para jóvenes? |
| camp sites? | los campings? |
| Do you find accommodation for visitors? | ¿Buscan ustedes alojamiento para los visitantes? |
| I want a first-class/second class hotel. | Quiero un hotel de primera clase/segunda clase. |
| a pension. | una pensión. |
| a double room. | un cuarto doble. |
| just a single room. | sólo un cuarto sencillo. |
| We'll go right away. How do I get there? | Vamos inmediatamente. ¿Cómo voy ahí? |

## At Airports

| | |
|---|---|
| Where is the check-in desk? | ¿Dónde está el mostrador de salida? |
| Can I take this in the cabin? | ¿Puedo llevar esto en la cabina? |
| Do I have to pay excess? | ¿Tengo que pagar exceso? |
| You haven't given me a luggage claim stub. | No me ha dado la contraseña del equipaje. |
| I've missed my flight. Can you give me another one? | He perdido mi vuelo. Me puede dar otro? |
| Is there a bar after customs check? | ¿Hay un bar pasando la aduana? |
| Where is the flight indicator? | ¿Dónde está el indicador de vuelos? |
| Is there a duty-free shop? | ¿Hay una tienda libre de impuestos? |
| Is there another way to go up/down other than by escalator? | ¿Hay otro modo de subir/bajar aparte de la escalera eléctrica? |
| Where can I get flight insurance? | ¿Dónde puedo obtener un seguro de vuelo? |
| Is there a wheel chair available? | ¿Hay una silla de ruedas disponible? |
| Is the flight delayed? | ¿Viene retrasado el vuelo? |
| At what time do we land? | ¿A qué hora aterrizamos? |

## At the Railway Stations

| | |
|---|---|
| Where is the ticket office? | ¿Dónde está la oficina de boletos? |

# Airports, Terminals and Stations

| | |
|---|---|
| One first-class/second-class return ticket to Mexico City. | **Un boleto de primera clase/ segunda clase de viaje redondo a la Ciudad de México.** |
| on the express. | **en el expreso.** |
| direct. | **directo.** |
| How much is the ticket? | **¿Cuánto vale el boleto?** |
| How much is a child's fare? | **¿Cuánto vale un boleto de niño?** |
| Can I reserve a seat/berth/ compartment? | **¿Puedo reservar un asiento/ una litera/un gabinete?** |
| Is there a supplement to pay? | **¿Hay que pagar suplemento?** |
| Do I have to change? | **¿Tengo que transbordar?** |
| Will there be a diner on the train? | **¿Habrá coche-comedor en el tren?** |
| Where must I change? | **¿Dónde tengo que transbordar?** |
| Where is the platform for the train to Monterrey? | **¿Dónde está el andén para el tren a Monterrey?** |
| Does my friend need a platform ticket? | **¿Necesita mi amigo un boleto de andén?** |
| What time does the train leave? | **¿A qué hora sale el tren?** |

## At a Port

| | |
|---|---|
| Which is pier number six? | **¿Cuál es el muelle número seis?** |
| At what time can I go on board? | **¿A qué hora puedo ir a bordo?** |
| Will there be an announcement when visitors must disembark? | **¿Habrá un anuncio cuando las visitas deban desembarcar?** |

## VOCABULARY

| | |
|---|---|
| bench | el banco |
| bus driver | el conductor |
| clock | el reloj |
| exit | la salida |
| gate | la entrada |
| guard | el vigilante |
| lockers | los casilleros |
| porter | el maletero |
| security officer | el oficial de seguridad |
| station master | el jefe de estación |
| loudspeaker | el altavoz |
| ticket collector | el conductor |
| vending machine | la máquina expendedora |
| waiting room | la sala de espera |

# En Route

## General Expressions

| | |
|---|---|
| At what time do we leave/take off? | ¿A qué hora salimos/despegamos? |
| Why is there a delay? | ¿Por qué hay retraso? |
| Have I got time to go to the bathroom? | ¿Tengo tiempo de ir al baño? |
| I have mislaid my ticket. | He perdido mi boleto. |
| Take my address and passport number. | Tome mi dirección y el número de mi pasaporte. |
| Is this seat reserved? | ¿Está reservado este asiento? |

## Travelling by Air

| | |
|---|---|
| Are you the stewardess? | ¿Es usted la azafata? |
| Which button do I press to call you? | Qué botón aprieto para llamarle? |
| Can you help me to adjust my seat? | ¿Puede ayudarme a ajustar mi asiento? |
| Shall I fasten my seat belt? | ¿Abrocho mi cinturón? |
| I haven't got a sick bag. | No tengo una bolsa de papel. |
| How high are we flying? | ¿A qué altura volamos? |
| What speed are we flying at? | ¿A qué velocidad vamos? |
| What town is that down there? | ¿Qué pueblo es ese de abajo? |
| Is there a map of the route? | ¿Hay un mapa de la ruta? |
| Are there any duty-free goods available? | ¿Hay artículos libres de impuestos? |

| | |
|---|---|
| Can I pay you in foreign money?<br>American money? | ¿Puedo pagar en moneda extranjera?<br>dinero americano? |
| The airvent is stuck. | El conducto de aire está bloqueado. |
| May I change my seat? | ¿Puedo cambiar mi asiento? |

## VOCABULARY

| | |
|---|---|
| airplane | el avión |
| airport | el aeropuerto |
| arrival gate | la llegada de viajeros |
| ashtray | el cenicero |
| flight deck | la cubierta de vuelo |
| fuselage | el fuselaje |
| jet engine | el reactor |
| light | la luz |
| luggage shelf | el portaequipajes |
| propeller | la hélice |
| tail | la cola |
| tray meal | la comida en bandeja |
| window | la ventanilla |
| wing | el ala |

## SIGNS

| | |
|---|---|
| Fasten your seat belt. | Abróchense los cinturones. |
| Emergency Exit | Salida de emergencia |
| No smoking | Prohibido fumar |

31

# Travelling

## Travelling by Rail

| | |
|---|---|
| Can you tell me where train number five is? | ¿Puede decirme dónde está el vagón número cinco? |
| I have a sleeping-berth reservation. | Tengo una reservación de litera. |
| This is my seat reservation. | Esta es mi reservación de asiento. |
| Is this seat taken? | ¿Está ocupado este asiento? |
| Is the dining car at the front or the back? | ¿Está el carro comedor delante o detrás? |
| Two tickets on the first train out, please. | Dos boletos para la primera salida, por favor. |
| Is the diner open throughout the journey? | ¿Está el carro comedor abierto todo el tiempo? |
| Can I leave my big suitcase in the baggage car? | ¿Puedo dejar mi maleta grande en el carro de equipaje? |
| Is there an observation car? | ¿Hay un carro-mirador? |
| What station is this? | ¿Qué estación es ésta? |
| The heating is on/off; too high/too low. | La calefacción está prendida apagada demasiado alta/ demasiado baja. |
| The air conditioning is on/off; too high/too low. | El aire acondicionado está encendido/apagado demasiado alto/demasiado bajo. |
| I can't open/close the window. | No puedo abrir/cerrar la ventana. |
| Where do I have to change? | ¿Dónde tengo que transbordar? |
| Is this where I get my connection for Veracruz? | ¿Es aquí donde tomo la conexión para Veracruz? |

## VOCABULARY

| | |
|---|---|
| blanket | la manta |
| corridor | el pasillo |
| compartment | el gabinete |
| cushion | la almohada |
| luggage rack | la rejilla |
| non smoking | prohibido fumar |
| sleeping berth | la litera |
| sleeping car | el carro dormitorio |
| sliding door | la puerta corrediza |

## SIGNS

| | |
|---|---|
| Do not lean out of the window. | **Es peligroso asomarse.** |
| Do not use the toilet while the train is stationary. | **No utilice el baño cuando el tren esté parado.** |

## Travelling on a Ship

| | |
|---|---|
| Where is the purser's office? | **¿Dónde está la oficina del sobrecargo?** |
| Please will you show me to my cabin? | **¿Por favor, me puede llevar a mi cabina?** |
| Are you the steward? | **¿Es usted el camarero?** |
| Is there a children's nursery/a shop/a gymnasium? | **¿Hay una guardería de niños/una tienda/un gimnasio?** |
| Where can I get some seasick tablets? | **¿Dónde puedo obtener pastillas para el mareo?** |
| On which side do we disembark? | **¿En qué lado desembarcamos?** |
| The sea is calm/rough. | **El mar está en calma/agitado.** |

# Travelling

| | |
|---|---|
| What are those birds? | ¿Qué son esos pájaros? |
| Seagulls? | ¿Gaviotas? |

## VOCABULARY

| | |
|---|---|
| aft | la popa |
| anchor | el ancla |
| bridge | el puente |
| captain | el capitán |
| crew | la tripulación |
| deck | la cubierta |
| funnel | la chimenea |
| lifebelt | el salvavidas |
| lifeboat | el bote salvavidas |
| mast | el mástil |
| officer | el oficial |
| port (harbor) | el puerto |
| port (left) | el babor |
| propeller | la hélice |
| radar | el radar |
| raft | la balsa |
| rail | el barandal |
| starboard | el estribor |

## SIGNS

**Danger - Propellers**
**Peligro - Hélices**

# Travelling by Coach (Limousine)

| | |
|---|---|
| Is this the coach for Puebla? | ¿Es este el camión (limousine) a Puebla? |
| Can I sit near the driver? | ¿Puedo sentarme cerca del conductor? |
| Are the seats numbered? | ¿Están los asientos numerados? |

| | |
|---|---|
| Do I pay on the coach? | ¿Pago dentro del camión? |
| How often does it stop? | ¿Cuántas paradas hace? |
| Would you mind closing the windows? It's drafty. | ¿Le importa cerrar la ventana? Hay corriente. |
| Can you help me with my luggage? | ¿Me puede ayudar con mi equipaje? |

VOCABULARY

| | |
|---|---|
| back seat | el asiento de atrás |
| driver | el conductor |
| foot rest | el apoyapié |
| front seat | el asiento delantero |
| guide | el guía |
| luggage compartment | el compartimiento del equipaje |

## Buses and Subway

| | |
|---|---|
| Where is the bus stop? | ¿Dónde está la parada del autobús? |
| Does one have to form in line? | ¿Tiene uno que hacer fila? |
| Do you go by the Alameda? | ¿Pasa usted por la Alameda? |
| Will you tell me when we reach Juarez Avenue? | ¿Me puede avisar cuando lleguemos a la Avenida Juárez? |
| I want to get off at the next stop. | Quiero bajar en la próxima parada. |
| Will you ring the bell please? | ¿Puede tocar el timbre por favor? |
| I want to go to the Zócalo. | Quiero ir al Zócalo. |
| Which line do I take? | ¿Qué línea tomo? |

**35**

# Travelling

| | |
|---|---|
| Do I have to change? | ¿Tengo que transbordar? |
| At what time is the last subway train? | ¿A qué hora es el último metro? |
| Here is a subway plan. | Aquí tiene un mapa del metro. |
| bus | Camión (de pasajeros) |
| truck | Camión (de carga) |

## VOCABULARY

| | |
|---|---|
| Automatic doors | las puertas automáticas |
| barrier | la barrera |
| escalator | la escalera eléctrica |

## Other Vehicles

| | |
|---|---|
| Where can I hire a bicycle? a motorbike? | ¿Dónde puedo alquilar una bicicleta? una motocicleta? |
| Please put air in this tire. | Por favor, infle esta llanta. |
| One of the spokes is broken. | Uno de los radios está roto. |
| The brake is not working. | El freno no funciona. |
| Do you have a bicycle with gears? | ¿Tiene una bicicleta con velocidades? |
| The seat needs lowering/raising. | El asiento necesita bajar/subir. |
| Are there any horse-drawn vehicles at this resort? | ¿Hay algún vehículo tirado por caballos en este lugar? |
| Will you put the roof down, please? | ¿Puede bajar la tapa, por favor? |
| Can the children sit with the driver? | ¿Pueden los niños sentarse con el conductor? |
| Please adjust the safety belt for me. | Por favor, ajuste el cinturón de seguridad para mí. |

36

| | |
|---|---|
| Do they run frequently? | ¿Funcionan muy a menudo? |
| Can I walk down? | ¿Puedo bajar andando? |
| Do you sell season tickets? | ¿Vende boletos de temporada? |

## VOCABULARY

| | |
|---|---|
| bicycle pump | la bomba de bicicleta |
| carrier | el portaequipajes |
| chain | la cadena |
| donkey | el burro |
| handlebar | el manubrio |
| harness | las guarniciones |
| light (of car, etc.) | el faro |
| mudguard | el guardabarros |
| pedal | el pedal |
| rear light | la luz trasera |
| skis | los esquíes |
| whip/crop | el látigo/el fuete |

## Walking About

IN TOWN

| | |
|---|---|
| Is this the main shopping street? | ¿Es ésta la calle principal? |
| Where is the town hall/ police station? | ¿Dónde está el ayuntamiento/ delegación /comisaría? |
| Can you direct me to the tourist office? | ¿Podría indicarme dónde está la oficina de turismo? |
| In what part of town are the theatres/nightclubs? | ¿En qué parte de la ciudad están los teatros/centros nocturnos? |
| Can I get there by bus/ subway/taxi? | ¿Puedo ir allí en camión/ metro/taxi? |

# Travelling

| | |
|---|---|
| Is there a market in the town? | ¿Hay un mercado en la ciudad? |
| What day is market day? | ¿Qué día hay mercado? |
| Is the business center near? | ¿Está cerca el centro comercial? |
| Must one cross at the traffic lights? | ¿Debe uno cruzar en los semáforos de tráfico? |
| Do pedestrians have right of way here? | ¿Tienen los peatones derecho de paso aquí? |
| Is there a public toilet near? | ¿Hay un baño público cerca? |

## VOCABULARY

| | |
|---|---|
| castle | el castillo |
| cathedral | la catedral |
| cemetery | el panteón |
| church | la iglesia |
| city center | el centro |
| concert hall | la sala de conciertos |
| courts | el juzgado/la delegación |
| docks | los muelles |
| exhibition | la exposición |
| factory | la fábrica |
| fountain | la fuente |
| government buildings | los edificios de gobierno |
| gardens | los jardines |
| harbor | el puerto |
| lake | el lago |
| monastery | el monasterio |
| monument | el monumento |
| museum | el museo |
| old town | la ciudad antigua |
| opera house | el teatro de la ópera |
| palace | el palacio |
| park | el parque |
| ruins | las ruinas |

| | |
|---|---|
| shopping center | el centro comercial |
| stadium | el estadio |
| statue | la estatua |
| stock exchange | la bolsa |
| subway | el metro |
| traffic lights | los semáforos |
| tower | la torre |
| university | la universidad |
| zoo | el zoológico |

IN THE COUNTRY

| | |
|---|---|
| May I walk through here? | ¿Puedo pasar por aquí? |
| Is this a public footpath? | ¿Es ésta una vereda pública? |
| Do I need permission to fish? | ¿Necesito permiso para pescar? |
| Which way is north/south/east/west? | ¿Qué camino es al norte/sur/este/oeste? |
| Is there a bridge or ford across this stream? | ¿Hay un puente o vado a través de este arroyo? |
| How far is the nearest village? | ¿A qué distancia está el pueblo más cercano? |
| I am lost. Can you please direct me to. . .? | Me he perdido. ¿Puede indicarme el camino a. . .? |
| Will you please show me the route on this map? | ¿Me puede enseñar el camino en este mapa, por favor? |

VOCABULARY

| | |
|---|---|
| barn | el granero |
| bird | el pájaro |
| brook | el arroyo |
| canal | el canal |
| cliff | el acantilado |
| cottage | la cabaña |

| | |
|---|---|
| cow | la vaca |
| dog | el perro |
| farm | la granja |
| field | el prado |
| footpath | la vereda |
| forest | el bosque |
| goat | la cabra |
| heath | el breñal |
| hill | la colina |
| horse | el caballo |
| inn | el mesón |
| lake | el lago |
| marsh | el pantano |
| moorland | el páramo |
| mountain | la montaña |
| orchard | la huerta |
| peak | el pico |
| pond | el estanque |
| river | el río |
| sea | el mar |
| sheep | la oveja |
| spring | la fuente |
| stream | el arroyo |
| tree | el árbol |
| valley | el valle |
| village | el pueblo |
| vineyard | la viña |
| waterfall | la cascada |
| well | el pozo |
| woods | el bosque |

# MOTORING

## At the Border

| | |
|---|---|
| Here is my car registration. | Aquí está mi certificado de matrícula. |
| insurance. | seguro. |

| | |
|---|---|
| driving license. | licencia de manejar / conducir. |
| I have an international license. | Tengo una licencia internacional. |
| This is a translation of my license. | Esta es una traducción de mi licencia norteamericana. |
| This is a rented car. Here are the documents. | Este es un coche alquilado. Aquí están los documentos. |
| You want to open the trunk? | ¿Quiére abrir la cajuela? |
| I arrived today. | He llegado hoy. |
| I am staying for two weeks. | Me quedo dos semanas. |
| We are passing through on the way to Guatemala. | Estamos de paso, camino a Guatemala. |
| Does this customs post close at night? | ¿Cierra por la noche este puesto de aduana? |
| At what time? | ¿A qué hora? |
| Shall I leave my engine running? | ¿Dejo el motor en marcha? |
| Do you want me to stop the engine? | ¿Quiére que pare el motor? |

## On the Road

**Mexico City** is the hub of the country. There are several excellent highways from the capital to other cities such as **Querétaro**, **Acapulco** and **Puebla**, as well as the Panamerican Highway to the border. These roads pass through many small sleepy towns which appear to be deserted. The high walls around the dwellings give them that effect.

| | |
|---|---|
| Can you tell me how to get to **Taxco**? | ¿Puede decirme cómo se va a Taxco? |

# Motoring

| | |
|---|---|
| How many kilometers is it? | ¿Cuántos kilómetros hay? |
| Is it a good road? | ¿Es una buena carretera? |
| Is it hilly/flat/straight/winding? | ¿Es montañoso/llano/derecho/sinuoso? |
| What is the speed limit on this section? | ¿Cuál es el límite de velocidad en este tramo? |
| Will you point out the route on this map please? | ¿Me puede señalar la ruta en este mapa, por favor? |
| How much does this section of the toll road cost? | ¿Cuánto cuesta este tramo de la autopista? |
| Do I pay at the exit? | ¿Pago a la salida? |
| I'm sorry. I have no change. | Lo siento. No tengo cambio. |
| How far is it to the next gas station? | ¿A qué distancia está la próxima gasolinera? |
| I want twenty-five liters, please. | Quiero veinticinco litros, por favor. |
| Give me fifty pesos' worth. | Deme lo que sean cincuenta pesos. |
| Fill her up. | Llénelo. |
| Please check the oil and water. | Favor de revisar el aceite y el agua. |
| I need some air in the tires. | Necesito aire en las llantas. |
| I think the windshield water tank needs refilling. | Creo que el depósito de agua para limpiar el parabrisas necesita rellenarse. |
| Have you any distilled water for the battery? | ¿Tiene agua destilada para la batería? |
| Please clean the windshield. | Por favor limpie el parabrisas. |
| Have you any paper towels? | ¿Tiene toallas de papel? |
| Have you got a carwash? | ¿Tiene lavado de coches? |

| Can I park here? | ¿Puedo estacionar aquí? |
| Where is the nearest garage? | ¿Dónde está el estacionamiento más cercano? |

## Trouble with the Police

Usually the police are polite and helpful to visitors, but they are more likely to be so if you appear friendly and cooperative.

A few phrases in their language can sometimes work miracles.

| I'm sorry. I didn't see you signal. | Lo siento. No le ví señalar. |
| I thought I had right of way. | Creí que tenía el derecho de paso. |
| I apologize. I won't do it again. | Discúlpeme. No lo volveré a hacer. |
| Here is my name and address. | Aquí está mi nombre y dirección. |
| This is my passport. | Este es mi pasaporte. |
| Do I have to pay a fine? | ¿Tengo que pagar una multa? |
| How much? | ¿Cuánto? |
| I haven't got any cash on me. Can I settle up at the police station? | No llevo dinero. Puedo pagar en la delegación de policía? |
| Thank you for your courtesy. | Gracias por ser tan amable. |

## Car Rental

| I want to hire a small car. | Quiero alquilar un coche pequeño. |

| | |
|---|---|
| a family sedan. | un sedán. |
| a large car. | un coche grande. |
| a sports car. | un coche deportivo. |
| a van. | una camioneta. |
| I shall need it for. . . days. | Lo necesitaré por. . . días. |
| How much is the daily charge? | ¿Cuánto cuesta por día? |
| Is it cheaper by the week? | ¿Es más barato por semana? |
| Does that include mileage and insurance? | ¿Incluye el kilometraje y el seguro? |
| What is the mileage charge? | ¿Cuánto es por el kilometraje? |
| Is the insurance for car and passengers? | ¿Es el seguro para el coche y los pasajeros? |
| Where do I pick up the car? | ¿Dónde recojo el coche? |
| Can you bring it to my hotel? | ¿Lo puede traer a mi hotel? |
| Can I leave it at another town or at the airport? | ¿Puedo dejarlo en otra ciudad o en el aeropuerto? |
| Is there a deposit to pay? | ¿Hay que pagar un depósito? |
| May I pay with my credit card? | ¿Puedo pagar con mi tarjeta de crédito? |
| Will you check the documents with me, please? | ¿Puede revisar los documentos conmigo, por favor? |
| Will you show me the gears and instrument panel? | ¿Me enseña la caja de velocidades y el tablero de instrumentos? |
| Is the tank full of gas? | ¿Está el tanque lleno de gasolina? |

## Road Signs

| | |
|---|---|
| Customs | **Aduana** |
| Stop | **Alto** |
| Parking | **Estacionamiento** |
| Warning | **Atención** |
| Toll Road | **Autopista** |
| Bad surface | **Camino deteriorado** |
| Narrow embankments | **Cuneta angosta** |
| Give way | **Ceda el paso** |
| Road interrupted | **Camino cortado** |
| City center | **Centro** |
| Dangerous crossing | **Cruce peligroso** |
| Warning | **Cuidado** |
| Dangerous curve | **Curva peligrosa** |
| Slow | **Despacio** |
| Detour | **Desviación** |
| One way | **Un solo sentido** |
| School | **Escuela** |
| Parking forbidden | **Estacionamiento prohibido** |
| Limited time parking | **Estacionamiento con límite de tiempo** |
| Road under repairs | **Camino en reparación** |
| Flyover | **Paso a desnivel** |
| Pedestrians | **Peatones** |
| No overtaking | **Prohibido rebasar** |

## Trouble on the Road

OTHER PEOPLE'S

| | |
|---|---|
| There has been an accident three miles back. | Ha habido un accidente a cinco kilómetros de aquí. |
| Will you phone the police, please? | ¿Puede llamar a la policía, por favor? |
| No, I did not see it happen. | No. No he visto como ha sucedido. |

## Motoring

|  |  |
|---|---|
| The car number was. . . | El número del coche era. . . |
| I do not think anyone is hurt. | No creo que haya heridos. |
| Someone is badly hurt. | Alguien está malherido. |

YOURS

|  |  |
|---|---|
| Are you all right? | ¿Está usted bien? |
| My passengers are not hurt. | Mis pasajeros no están heridos. |
| The car is damaged. | Mi coche ha sufrido daños. |
| May I have your insurance details? | ¿Me puede dar los datos de su seguro? |
| Your name and address, please? | ¿Su nombre y dirección, por favor? |
| I think we shall have to call the police. | Creo que tendremos que llamar a la policía. |
| Excuse me, would you mind being a witness? | Perdone, ¿le importa ser testigo? |
| It happened because he stepped on his brakes suddenly. | Ha ocurrido porque aplicó los frenos repentinamente. |
| He came out of a side road without signalling. | Salió de una calle secundaria sin hacer señal. |
| He tried to pass me on a narrow stretch of road. | Trató de rebasarme en un tramo angosto. |
| He turned off without signalling. | Dio vuelta sin hacer señal. |
| May I explain to someone who understands English? | ¿Puedo explicarme a alguien que entienda el inglés? |

If you are unfortunate enough to have an accident, be sure to get all the details from the other driver involved. Your insurance company will have provided you with an accident report form. Fill it in on the spot with the help of the other driver. Above all, keep cool.

## Breakdown

| | |
|---|---|
| Thank you for stopping. I am in trouble. Will you help me? | Gracias por pararse. Estoy en un apuro. ¿Me puede ayudar? |
| My car has broken down. | Mi coche está averiado. |
| Will you tell the next garage or breakdown service vehicle that you pass? | ¿Se lo puede decir al próximo garage o taller de mecánico que pase? |
| Will you please telephone a garage for me? | ¿Puede telefonear a un garage por mí, por favor? |
| Can you give me a lift to the next telephone? | ¿Me puede llevar en su coche hasta el próximo teléfono? |
| Can you send a breakdown truck? | ¿Puede enviar una camioneta de socorro? |
| I am five kilometers from the last exit. | Estoy a cinco kilómetros de la última salida. |
| I am three kilometers from Cuernavaca on the old road. | Estoy a tres kilómetros de Cuernavaca, en el camino viejo. |
| How long will you be? | ¿Cuánto tardará? |

## Repairs

| | |
|---|---|
| There's something wrong with the engine. | Hay algo que no va bien en el motor. |
| The clutch is slipping. | El clutch está patinando. |
| There is a noise in the back. | Hay un ruído en la parte de atrás. |
| The brakes are not working. | Los frenos no funcionan. |
| The cooling system is leaking. | El sistema de enfriamiento gotea. |
| I've got a flat tire. | Tengo una llanta ponchada. |

# Motoring

| | |
|---|---|
| My fan belt is broken. | La banda del ventilador está rota. |
| The electrical system has failed. | El sistema eléctrico ha fallado. |
| The engine is overheating. | El motor se calienta demasiado. |
| The car won't start. | El coche no arranca. |
| What is the matter? | ¿Qué pasa? |
| Is it broken? | ¿Está roto? |
|    burnt out? |    quemado? |
|    disconnected? |    desconectado? |
|    jammed? |    trabado? |
|    leaking? |    goteando? |
|    short circuiting? |    con corto circuito? |
| Do I need a new part? | ¿Necesito una refacción? |
| Is there a Ford agency in town? | ¿Hay una agencia Ford en la ciudad? |
| Can you send for the part? | ¿Puede pedir la pieza? |
| Is it serious? | ¿Es grave? |
| How long will it take to repair? | ¿Cuánto tiempo tardará en repararlo? |
| Can I hire another car? | ¿Puedo alquilar otro coche? |
| What will it cost? | ¿Cuánto costará? |
| I will get the part flown from the United States. | Haré que manden por avión la pieza desde los Estados Unidos. |
| Your mechanic has been very kind; I would like to tip him. | Su mecánico ha sido muy amable; me gustaría darle una propina. |

## VOCABULARY

| | |
|---|---|
| battery | la batería |
| brakes | los frenos |
| brake lining | la guarnición del freno |
| bulbs | las bombillas |
| carburetor | el carburador |
| clutch | el clutch |
| cooling system | sistema de enfriamiento |
| parking lights | las luces bajas |
| dynamo | la dínamo |
| distributor | el distribuidor |
| electrical system | el sistema eléctrico |
| engine | el motor |
| exhaust pipe | el tubo de escape |
| fan | la ventilación |
| filter | el filtro |
| fuel pump | la bomba de gasolina |
| fuel tank | el tanque |
| gears | la caja de velocidades |
| generator | el generador |
| hand brake | el freno de mano |
| head lights | los faros |
| heating system | la calefacción |
| horn | el claxon |
| ignition | el switch |
| indicator | el indicador |
| lubrication system | el sistema de lubricación |
| radiator | el radiador |
| reflectors | los reflectores |
| seat | el asiento |
| silencer | el silenciador |
| spark plug | la bujía |
| speedometer | el indicador de velocidad |
| suspension | la suspensión |
| transmission | la transmisión |
| wheels | las ruedas |
| windshield wipers | el limpiaparabrisas |

49

# A Place to Stay

There are places to stay to suit every budget level in Mexico and Latin America, from first-class hotels to simple pensions. If you have not booked a hotel in advance, ask at the tourist office of each town. They will help you find a place within your price range. If you don't want to stay at a hotel, there are apartments and rooms in private houses. The standards of comfort vary considerably and cheap accommodation is often rather austere.

## Hotels and Pensions

### Finding a Room

| | |
|---|---|
| I am travelling with the. . . Travel Agency. | Viajo con la Agencia. . . |
| Here is my hotel reservation. | Aquí está mi reservación para el hotel. |
| My room is already reserved. | Mi habitación ya está reservada. |
| I am travelling independently. | Viajo independientemente. |
| Will a bell boy bring my luggage in? | ¿Me puede traer un mozo el equipaje? |
| Can I leave my car here? | ¿Puedo dejar mi coche aquí? |
| Is there parking? | ¿Hay estacionamiento? |
| Are you the desk clerk/ manager? | ¿Es usted la recepcionista/el gerente? |
| Have you a single/double/ three-bedded room? | ¿Tiene una habitación sencilla/doble/de tres camas? |
| with bathroom? | con baño? |
| with bath or shower? | con baño o regadera? |
| with a balcony? | con balcón? |
| with a steet view? | con vista a la calle? |

| | |
|---|---|
| How much is it per day? | ¿Cuánto es por día? |
| Is there a reduction for a longer stay/for children? | ¿Hay rebaja por una estancia más larga/por niños? |
| Are there special mealtimes for children? | ¿Hay horas de comer especiales para niños? |
| I don't want to pay more than . . .pesos a day. | No quiero pagar más de. . . pesos diario. |
| Have you anything cheaper? | ¿Tiene algo más barato? |
| Must I fill a registration card? | ¿Tengo que llenar una tarjeta de registro? |
| Here is my passport. | Aquí está mi pasaporte. |
| How long will you keep it? | ¿Cuánto tiempo lo tendrá? |
| I'd like to go up to my room right away. | Me gustaría ir a mi habitación inmediatamente. |
| Will you send up the luggage? | ¿Me mandará el equipaje? |
| This valise is for Room 3 and that one for number 12. | Esta maleta es para la habitación tres y la otra para el número doce. |
| May I have the key? | ¿Me da la llave? |
| Is the key in the door? | ¿Está la llave en la puerta? |
| Where is the elevator? | ¿Dónde está el elevador? |
| Do I work it myself? | ¿Es automático? |
| Do you do bed and breakfast/demi pension? | ¿Dan cama y desayuno/media pensión? |
| Can I put all extras on my bill? | ¿Puedo cargar todos los extras en mi cuenta? |
| Is there a mail box in the hotel? | ¿Hay un buzón en el hotel? |
| Can you get the daily papers for me? | ¿Puede conseguir los periódicos para mí? |

# Accommodation

## Moving in

This room is too small/large/noisy/dark/high up.

Este cuarto es demasiado pequeño/grande/ruidoso/obscuro/alto.

You haven't got a double bed?

¿No tiene una cama doble?

Please make the twin beds into one double.

Por favor, convierta las dos camas en una doble.

I need a child's cot.

Necesito una cuna de niño.

I'll need another pillow/blanket/clothes hanger/writing paper.

Necesitaré otra almohada/manta/gancho para ropa/papel de escribir.

The bedside light is not working.

La lámpara del lado de la cama no funciona.

The bulb is blown.

El foco está fundido.

Which is the faucet for the hot/cold water?

¿Cuál es la llave del agua caliente/fría?

Is this the electric razor socket?

¿Es éste el enchufe de la máquina de afeitar?

What is the voltage?

¿Cuál es el voltaje?

My plug won't fit.

Mi clavija no sirve.

Have you got an adaptor?

¿Tiene un adaptador?

Is there an electrician in town?

¿Hay un electricista en el pueblo?

Is there a hotel laundry/facilities for washing and ironing clothes?

¿Hay lavandería en el hotel/facilidades para lavar y planchar la ropa?

The blind is stuck.

La persiana está trabada.

Will you bring a bottle of drinking water?

¿Puede traer una botella de agua potable?

| | |
|---|---|
| Can I leave valuables in the hotel safe? | ¿Puedo dejar mis valores en la caja fuerte del hotel? |
| What time is breakfast/ lunch/dinner? | ¿A qué hora es el desayuno/ la comida/cena? |
| Do you serve breakfast in the room? | ¿Sirven desayuno en la habitación? |
| Does the hotel make box lunches? | ¿Hace el hotel cajas de lunch para llevar? |

## Small Hotels and Pensions

| | |
|---|---|
| Do you have set times for meals? | ¿Tiene horas fijas para las comidas? |
| May I have a towel and soap? | ¿Puede darme una toalla y jabón? |
| At what time do you lock up at night? | ¿A qué hora cierra la puerta por la noche? |
| May I have a key? | ¿Me da la llave? |
| Is it all right to leave the car in the street? | ¿Está bien si dejo el coche en la calle? |
| Will our things be safe? | ¿Estarán seguras nuestras cosas? |
| Where is the nearest garage? | ¿Cuál es el garage más cercano? |

## Rooms in Private Houses

| | |
|---|---|
| Do you have a free room? | ¿Tiene una habitación libre? |
| Do you serve breakfast? | ¿Dan desayuno? |
| Is there a café nearby? | ¿Hay un café cerca? |
| Would you like me to pay now? | ¿Quiére que pague ahora? |

## Accommodation

| | |
|---|---|
| At what time will it be convenient to use the bathroom? | ¿A qué hora le viene bien que use el baño? |
| Do I have to tell you when I take a bath? | ¿Se lo tengo que decir si me doy un baño? |
| Could you wake us in the morning? | ¿Nos puede despertar en la mañana? |
| Is there a lounge? | ¿Hay un salón? |
| Shall I lock my room? | ¿Cierro mi puerta con llave? |

## Paying the Bill

| | |
|---|---|
| May I have my bill, please? | ¿Me da la cuenta, por favor? |
| Will you prepare my bill for first thing tomorrow? | ¿Me preparará la cuenta para mañana a primera hora? |
| I think there is a mistake. | Creo que hay un error. |
| I don't understand this item. | No entiendo este detalle. |
| May I pay by check? | ¿Puedo pagar con cheque? |
| Do you accept credit cards? | ¿Aceptan tarjetas de crédito? |
| Is service included? | ¿Está incluido el servicio? |
| Is tax included? | ¿Están incluidos los impuestos? |
| May I have a receipt, please? | ¿Me da un recibo, por favor? |
| Please forward my mail to. . . | Por favor, remita mi correspondencia a. . . |
| We have enjoyed ourselves very much. | Lo hemos disfrutado mucho. |
| May I have one of your leaflets? | ¿Me da uno de sus folletos? |

VOCABULARY

| | |
|---|---|
| bar | el bar |
| barman | el cantinero |
| bed | la cama |
| chair | la silla |
| chambermaid | la recamarera |
| children's playground | el patio de recreo de niños |
| discotheque | la discoteca |
| door | la puerta |
| hall | el vestíbulo |
| elevator | el elevador |
| lounge | el salón |
| light switch | el apagador |
| bellboy | el maletero |
| manager | el gerente |
| mirror | el espejo |
| night club | el club nocturno |
| playground | el patio |
| radio | el radio |
| restaurant | el restorán |
| stairs | las escaleras |
| swimming pool | la alberca |
| telephone operator | la telefonista |
| waiter | el mesero / camarero |
| waitress | la mesera / camarera |
| wardrobe closet | el ropero / armario |
| window | la ventana |

# Catering for Yourself

## Villas and Apartments

| | |
|---|---|
| I have booked a villa/ apartment. | He reservado una villa/un departamento. |
| Here is my voucher. | Aquí está mi vale. |

# Catering for Yourself

| | |
|---|---|
| Will you please show me around? | Por favor, ¿me lo enseña? |
| Where is the light switch/fuse box? | ¿Dónde está el apagador/la caja de fusibles? |
| Do all the outside doors lock? | ¿Cierran con llave todas las puertas exteriores? |
| Will you show me the hot water system? | ¿Me puede enseñar el sistema de agua caliente? |
| Where is the mains valve? | ¿Dónde está la válvula de la cañería? |
| Is there a gas main? | ¿Hay alimentación de gas? |
| Are gas cylinders delivered? | ¿Reparten los cilindros de gas? |
| At what time does the house help arrive? | ¿A qué hora viene la sirvienta? |
| Can we have three sets of keys? | ¿Nos puede dar tres juegos de llaves? |
| When is the rubbish collected? | ¿Cuándo recogen la basura? |
| Are there shops nearby? | ¿Hay tiendas cercas? |
| Where is the bus stop/station? | ¿Dónde está la parada/estación de autobús? |
| Have you a map of the place? | ¿Tiene un mapa del lugar? |

## Camping

| | |
|---|---|
| Have you a free site? | ¿Tiene un lugar libre? |
| Do you rent bungalows? tents? cooking equipment? | ¿Alquila bungalows? tiendas de campaña equipo de cocina? |
| Are there toilets? washing facilities? | ¿Hay baños? facilidades para lavarse? |

| | |
|---|---|
| cooking facilities? | facilidades para cocinar? |
| How much does it cost per night? | ¿Cuánto cuesta por noche? |
| Can I put my tent here? | ¿Puedo poner mi tienda de campaña aquí? |
| Is there room for a trailer? | ¿Hay espacio para un remolque? |
| Is there a night guard? | ¿Hay vigilancia de noche? |
| Where is the camp shop? | ¿Dónde está la tienda del camping? |
| restaurant? | el restorán? |
| the nearest shopping center? | el centro comercial más cercano? |
| At what time do we have to vacate the site? | ¿A qué hora tenemos que desocupar el sitio? |
| Where is the drinking faucet? | ¿Dónde está la llave del agua potable? |

## VOCABULARY

| | |
|---|---|
| barbecue | la barbacoa |
| basin | el lavabo |
| bucket | la cubeta/el cubo |
| camping gas | el gas butano |
| tent frame | la armazón de la tienda |
| grill | la parrilla |
| guyropes | las cuerdas |
| ice bucket | el cubo de hielo |
| insecticide | el insecticida |
| knife | el cuchillo |
| mosquito repellant | el repelente de mosquitos |
| penknife | la navaja |
| sleeping bag | la bolsa de dormir |
| spade | la pala |

# Catering for Yourself

| | |
|---|---|
| stove | **el hornillo** |
| tent | **la tienda de campaña** |
| tent peg | **la estaca** |
| waterproof sheet | **la sábana impermeable** |

## Youth Hostelling

| | |
|---|---|
| Is there a youth hostel in this town? | **¿Hay un albergue para jóvenes en esta ciudad?** |
| Have you room for tonight? | **¿Tiene una habitación para esta noche?** |
| We are members of the Youth Hostel Association. | **Somos miembros de la Sociedad de Albergues Juveniles.** |
| What are the house rules? | **¿Cuáles son las reglas del albergue?** |
| How long can we stay? | **¿Cuánto nos podemos quedar?** |
| Is there a youth hostel at. . .? | **¿Hay un albergue en. . .?** |

# Eating and Drinking

Mealtimes not only offer a chance to satisfy the appetite, but they provide an intimate glimpse of the life of the places you are visiting. There are the regional specialties to savour, which reveal something of the character of the local environment. The dishes of the Yucatan peninsula differ considerably from those of Puebla. Much depends on the geographical locality in the preparation of the various viands.

Above all, mealtimes provide an opportunity to watch the fascinating drama of people. . . the local residents as well as both national and international tourists. Different types of restaurants satisfy different tastes and there is an ample variety.

**Mexico** is a rich agricultural country and its food varies widely. There are many types of fruits and vegetables which are unknown in other parts of the world. There is much to enjoy, especially the fresh fish which can be obtained along the extensive Pacific coast, and the Gulf and Caribbean coastlines on the Atlantic side. Mealtimes in **Mexico** differ from those stateside. Breakfast is usually eaten at between 8:00 and 9:00 a.m.; dinner is served between 2:00 and 4:00 p.m., and supper about 8:00 p.m.

As is well-known, the basic foods of the common Mexican diet are rice, beans and tortillas, all prepared in myriad ways. Rice may be white (with diced vegetables; with diced cheese and pepper strips, etc.); red (based on tomato puree with diced vegetables, or with fried plantains, or with a sunny-side fried egg on top with jardiniere sauce, called here **salsa mexicana'**, etc.) or even green rice which has a watercress and **chili** base. Beans come in a variety of hues: the purple **flor de mayo**, the black **veracruzano**; yellow **canarios**; brownish **bayos**; white **alubias**; green and white **habas**. The **tortilla**, apart from its basic pancake shape served hot and brought to the table in a **chiquihuite** (special basket),

# Eating and Drinking

is the basic ingredient in many many dishes among which are soup, **garnachas, chalupas, chilaquiles, tacos, enchiladas, tostadas, pastel de Moctezuma, totopos,** etc.

As to some local beverages, **'aguas frescas'** (fresh waters) are taken with the meal. These are made of sugar, water and the juice of either lemon, soursop, orange, pineapple, cantaloupe melon, watermelon, papaya, and even from a concentrate of the **'jamaica'** flower. Much beer is consumed with meals. As to alcoholic beverages, there is **pulque, tequila, tepache,** and wine among others.

| | |
|---|---|
| Can you recommend a good restaurant? | **¿Puede recomendar un buen restorán?** |
| one that is not too expensive? | **uno que no sea demasiado caro?** |
| a typical restaurant of the region? | **un restorán típico de la región?** |
| one with music? | **uno con música?** |
| a first-class restaurant? | **un restorán de primera clase?** |
| a Chinese/Italian/French/Spanish restaurant? | **un restorán chino/italiano francés/español?** |
| Is there a good snack bar near? | **¿Hay cerca una buena fuente de sodas?** |
| Where can I find a self-service restaurant? | **¿Dónde puedo encontrar un restorán de autoservicio?** |
| Do I need to reserve a table? | **¿Necesito reservar una mesa?** |
| I'd like a table for two at nine o'clock. | **Quisiera una mesa para dos personas a las nueve.** |
| not too near the door/the orchestra. | **no demasiado cerca de la puerta/la orquesta.** |
| in the corner. | **en el rincón.** |
| away from the kitchen. | **a distancia de la cocina.** |

60

## At the Restaurant

| | |
|---|---|
| A table for four, please. | Una mesa para cuatro, por favor. |
| Is this our table? | ¿Es ésta nuestra mesa? |
| This table will do fine. | Esta mesa está bien. |
| The tablecloth is soiled. | El mantel está sucio. |
| The table is unsteady. | La mesa se mueve. |
| The ashtray is missing. | Falta el cenicero. |
| May I see the menu? | ¿Puedo ver el menú? |
| We will have a cocktail while we look at it. | Tomaremos un aperitivo mientras lo miramos. |
| Please bring the wine list. | Por favor, traiga la lista de vinos. |
| Have you got a set menu? | ¿Tiene un menú con comida del día? |
| What do you recommend today? | ¿Que recomienda hoy? |
| What does it consist of? | ¿De qué consiste? |
| It sounds good. I'll try it. | Parece bueno. Lo probaré. |
| The soup is cold. Please warm it up. | La sopa está fría. Por favor, caliéntela. |
| This fork is dirty. May I have a clean one? | Este tenedor está sucio. ¿Me puede dar uno limpio? |
| Will you call our waiter? | ¿Puede llamar a nuestro mesero? |
| We did not order this. | No pedimos esto. |
| I'd like to speak to the head waiter. | Quisiera hablar con el jefe. |

## Eating and Drinking

| | |
|---|---|
| My compliments to the chef. | **Saludos al cocinero.** |
| It's very good. | **Es muy bueno.** |
| Have you any house wine? | **¿Tiene vino de la casa?** |
| I'd like a half bottle/ a carafe. | **Me gustaría media botella/ una garrafa.** |
| Which is the local wine? | **¿Cuál es el vino local?** |
| This wine is corked. | **Este vino sabe a corcho.** |
| The children will share a portion. | **Los niños compartirán una porción.** |
| May we have some water? | **¿Nos puede traer agua?** |
| Have you any mineral water? | **¿Tiene agua mineral?** |
| Have you a high chair for the child? | **¿Tiene una silla alta para el niño?** |
| Where are the bathrooms? | **¿Dónde están los lavabos?** |

## The Menu

Menus will vary from place to place. Most restaurants have a set meal as well as a la carte. Tipping runs to between twelve and fifteen per cent of the bill.

### Appetizers

The serving of appetizers with the drink (or **'copa'**) is an old custom in Mexico. There is a wide variety of **'antojitos'** or **'botanas'** as they are also called. They may be either hot or cold.

| | |
|---|---|
| **Burritos** | Wheat tortillas, filled and rolled. |
| **Carnitas** | Small pieces of fried pork |

62

| | |
|---|---|
| **Chalupas** | Tortilla boats, of shredded pork or chicken, minced onions, tomato sauce and crumbled white cheese. |
| **Guacamole** | Avocado dip. |
| **Quesadillas** | Filled tortilla 'turnovers' |
| **Queso relleno** | Edam cheese filled with meat, steamed until runny and served with tortillas. |
| **Sopes, garnachas** | Small rounded tortilla batter, filled and garnished. |
| **Tacos** | Warm tortilla filled with shredded meat and topped with sauce. |
| | Also, tortilla filled with meat and fried, then topped with sauce. |
| **Tostadas** | Fried tortilla onto which is piled: refried beans, chicken, lettuce, tomato, cheese, chili, sour cream. |
| **Totopos** | Small crisp tortilla triangles used for dipping. |

In the preparation of the above foods, several native instruments are employed:

| | |
|---|---|
| **Molinillo** | a wooden, carved hand beater for making hot chocolate drink. |
| **Comal** | a cast iron griddle for making tortillas and appetizers. |
| **Metate** | a sloping rectangular piece of volcanic rock supported on three stout legs and having a long round rock 'mano' or roller. |

## Eating and Drinking

| | |
|---|---|
| | Used to grind corn, chilies and cacao. An 'Aztec blender'. |
| Molcajete | a pestle and mortar . . . of porous volcanic rock on three short legs. Used to crush ingredients to make sauces. |
| Chiquihuite | a basket for tortillas. |

It is interesting to note that these latter three words are not Spanish nor derivatives of a romance language, but rather are indigenous expressions. These instruments have been in use for over 3,500 years in the preparation of food.

Also worth mentioning is that Mexico, famous for its 'hot' food, has about two hundred different types of chilies. The most commonly used are: ancho, cascabel, cayenne, chilaca, chipotle, cuaresmeño, guajillo, habanero, jalapeño, mulato, pasilla, poblano, serrano, piquín, etc. Not all chilies are hot.

## Soups

| | |
|---|---|
| Sopa de aguacate | Avocado soup |
| Caldo tlalpeño | Vegetable broth |
| Sopa de elote y rajas | Fresh corn and chili soup |
| Sopa de flor de calabaza | Pumpkin blossom soup |
| Sopa de fideo | Noodle soup |
| Sopa de lima | Lime soup |
| Sopa de queso | Cheese soup |
| Sopa Tarasca | Tarascan bean and tomato soup |
| Sopa de tortilla | Tortilla soup |

## Stews

**Mole de olla**         Mole in a pot

**Pozole de Jalisco**    Pork and hominy soup

**Sopas secas** (dry soups) are served in Mexico. This might be
noodles with all the broth absorbed, topped with grated
cheese; or perhaps a rice dish with fried plantains or any
other combination.

## Meats

**Albóndigas de Jalisco**              Meat balls

**Albóndigas en salsa de
jitomate y chipotle**                  Meat balls in tomato and
                                       chipotle sauce

**Birria**                             Mutton or kid stew

**Bistecs rancheros**                  Country steaks

**Carne asada a la
Tampiqueña**                           Broiled meat in the Tampico
                                       style

**Carne claveatada**                   Pot roast with sprinkled
                                       almonds and bacon

**Chile relleno**                      Stuffed peppers

**Chile en Nogada**                    Chilies in walnut sauce.

The latter dish is difficult to classify as it contains not only
meat but vegetables, fruits and nuts. It was created by the
grateful people of Puebla who were giving a banquet in
honor of don Agustín de Iturbide's saint's day in 1821.
He had led the final revolt against Spanish domination. All the
dishes at the banquet were made of ingredients the colors of
the Mexican flag. Used in this dish were the **green** chilies,
the **white** sauce and the **red** pomegranate seeds. It is a great
delicacy and only obtainable during the harvesting time of
the walnut towards the end of September.

# Eating and Drinking

| | |
|---|---|
| **Cochinita pibil** | Barbecued suckling pig in sauce |
| **Estofado de lengua** | Stewed tongue |
| **Fiambre potosino** | Cold meats in a vinaigrette sauce |
| **Lomo de puerco adobado** | Spiced pork loin |
| **Puerco en mole verde** | Pork in green mole |

## Poultry and Game

| | |
|---|---|
| **Mole poblano** | Turkey in mole. The national dish. |
| **Pato en mole verde de pepita** | Duck in green mole made of pumpkin seeds |
| **Pollo en pipián rojo** | Chicken in red sesame sauce |
| **Pollo pibil** | Chicken barbecued in banana leaves. |

## Fish and Seafood

| | |
|---|---|
| **Cebiche** | Raw fish cocktail. . . marinated in lime juice. |
| **Jaibas rellenas** | Stuffed crabs |
| **Huachinango a la veracruzana** | Red snapper Veracruz style |
| **Pámpano en salsa verde** | Pompano in green sauce |
| **Pescado en cilantro** | Fish in coriander |
| **Pescado relleno** | Stuffed fish |
| **Pescado alcaparrado** | Fish in caper sauce |

## Vegetables

| | |
|---|---|
| **Budín de chícharo** | Pea pudding |
| **de Elote** | Green corn pudding |
| **de Zanahoria** | Carrot pudding |

| | |
|---|---|
| Calabacitas rellenas de elote | Zucchini squash stuffed with fresh corn |
| Calabacitas picadas con jitomate | Chopped zucchini and tomatoes |
| Chayotes rellenos | Vegetable pear, stuffed |
| Chile con queso | Chilies with cheese |
| Huazontles | Bunches of greens, spiked on top and thick with small green seeds |
| Rajas de chile poblano | Chili poblano strips |
| Torta de calabacitas | Zucchini squash torte |
| de Elote | Corn torte |
| de Garbanzos | Chickpea torte |

Beans, to which we have previously referred, are served in two basic manners: **'Frijoles de olla'** (beans in a pot) and **'Frijoles refritos'** (refried beans).

## Salads

| | |
|---|---|
| Ensalada de Nopalitos | Salad of diced nopal cactus |
| de Calabacita | Zucchini salad |
| de Jícama | Jicama salad. (Bulbous root of leguminous plant) |

## Eggs

| | |
|---|---|
| Huevos rancheros | Country style eggs. Fried, placed on a tortilla, topped with sauce. |
| Huevos revueltos a la mexicana | Eggs. Scrambled with tomato and chili. |
| Huevos con nopales | Eggs with diced nopal cactus |

# Eating and Drinking

## Desserts

| | |
|---|---|
| Ate con queso | Fruit paté eaten with cheese |
| Buñuelos | Fritters in anise-flavoured syrup |
| Cajeta de Celaya | Goats' milk dessert |
| Chongos zamoranos | Curds in syrup |
| Cocada imperial | Imperial coconut flan |
| Dulce de camote | Sweet Potato dessert |
| Flan a la antigua | Old fashioned flan |
| Guayabas rellenas con cocada | Guavas stuffed with coconut |
| Huevos reales | Egg sponge in syrup |
| Mangos flameados | Mango flambée |

Frequently imbibed is a sweet drink called 'atole'. It is a gruel mixed with fruit, usually pineapple or strawberries, and seasoned with chili. It is a natural accompaniment for tamales.

## Casserole Dishes

| | |
|---|---|
| Chilaquiles | Casserole of tortillas in a chili sauce |
| Enchiladas | Stuffed, folded tortilla in sauce |
| Papa-dzules | Tortillas in pumpkin seed sauce |
| Pastel de Moctezuma | Aztec pudding. . . tortillas, meat, cream, peppers, tomato sauce, cheese in layers and baked. |

68

**Tamales**

A sort of steamed dumpling served with sauce, wrapped in corn leaves. May be sweet. Tamales differ according to geographical location. Those of Oaxaca and Yucatan are wrapped in plantain leaves. In Michoacán, they are triangular shaped, wrapped in corn leaves and called 'corundas'.

## Wine

After the Conquest, the colonizers brought with them vines from Spain which they grafted on to an indigenous wild grape vine. These began to flourish on a small scale in the missions from Oaxaca to Baja California. The Spaniards feared that wines from New Spain might rival those produced in the mother country so in 1543, legislation was enacted to discourage their cultivation. Their death warrant was signed in a decree in 1771 which levied high penalties upon anyone growing vines or olives.

There has been a surge in recent years in the cultivation of grapes. Querétaro, Guanajuato, Aguascalientes and Baja California are steadily improving their products and some wines are surprisingly good.

## Beer

Beer, called **'cerveza'** in Mexico is consumed in enormous quantities. Mexican beer ranks among the finest in the world.

# Eating and Drinking

## Soft drinks

Coffee and hot chocolate are extensively consumed. Tea is brewed from an almost limitless variety of products: **Té negro** (black tea); **té de hojas de naranja** (orange leaf tea); **té de cabello de elote** (corn silk tea); **manzanilla** (camomile); **hierbabuena** (mint leaf); **flor de tila** (linden tree flower); **anís estrella** (anise); **zacate de limón** (lemon); etc., etc. Some are for medicinal uses.

The following is a list of specialty dishes found in the various provinces:

| | |
|---|---|
| **Aguascalientes** | **Albóndigas** (meat balls) |
| **Baja California** | **Macarela en leche** (mackerel in milk) |
| **Campeche** | **Pámpano campechano** (pompano local style) |
| **Coahuila** | **Rollo de nuez** (nut roll) |
| **Colima** | **Langostinos o camarones adobados** (Prawns or shrimp in adobo) |
| | **Cocada de Colima** (coconut dessert) |
| **Chiapas** | **Taquitos de plátano** (plantain tacos) |
| **Chihuahua** | **Picadillo** (chopped beef and pork with raisins, pine nuts) |
| **Durango** | **Enchiladas de Durango** (tortillas wrapped around some filling) |
| **Estado de Mexico** and the **Distrito Federal** | **Caldo tlalpeño** (beef broth with vegetables and chili) |

| | |
|---|---|
| | **Nopalitos con chipotle** (nopal cactus cooked with chipotle chili) |
| | **Huitlacoche con rajas** ( Corn fungus cooked with pepper slices, cream and cheese) |
| **Guanajuato** | **Gelatina de cajeta** (cooked and sweetened goat's milk dessert) |
| **Guerrero** | **Cebiche de Acapulco** (raw fish cocktail marinated in lime juice) |
| **Hidalgo** | **Palanquetas** (nut brittle candy) |
| **Jalisco** | **Pico de Gallo** (orange and jícama salad) |
| | **Pozole tapatío** (maize-based soup) |
| | **Pollo valentina** (chicken dish) |
| **Michoacán** | **Corundas** (dumplings in corn leaves, triangular-shaped, steamed and served with a sauce. |
| **Morelos** | **Lomo de cerdo con ciruelas** (Pork loin with prunes) |
| **Nayarit** | **Calabaza en piloncillo** (pumpkin in molasses) |
| **Nuevo León** | **Tamalitos de Nuevo León** (a sort of large dumpling wrapped in corn leaves) |
| **Oaxaca** | **Mole de olla** (pork, white beans, zucchini, green tomatoes) |

|  | **Tamales** (wrapped in plantain leaves) |
|---|---|
| **Puebla** | **Mole poblano** (a turkey in a spicy sauce including chocolate) |
|  | **Chiles en nogada** (gourmet fare. Stuffed peppers with fruits, walnut sauce and pomegranate garnish) |
| **Querétaro** | **Sopa de aguacate** (avocado soup) |
| **San Luis Potosí** | **Albóndigas de pobre** (pork meatballs) |
| **Sinaloa** | **Sopa de caguama** (turtle, corn, chili, onion, carrots, etc., soup) |
| **Sonora** | **Caldo de queso** (cheese soup) |
| **Tabasco** | **Plátanos rellenos** (stuffed plantains) |
| **Tamaulipas** | **Jaibas rellenas** (stuffed crab) |
| **Tlaxcala** | **Barbacoa en mixiote** (barbecued meat in a parchment wrapping) |
| **Veracruz** | **Huachinango a la veracruzana** (red snapper Veracruz style) |
|  | **Mole de pescado** (fish in piguant green sauce) |
| **Yucatán** | **Sopa de lima** (lime soup) |
|  | **Cochinita pibil** (suckling pig dish) |
|  | **Papa-dzul** (pumpkin seed sauce and tortilla) |

|  | **Queso relleno** (stuffed Edam cheese) |
| --- | --- |
| **Zacatecas** | **Chorizos con queso y chile** (spicy sausage with cheese and chili) |

## VOCABULARY

| | |
| --- | --- |
| **aceitunas** | olives |
| **achiote** | seed of the annatto tree |
| **acelgas** | spinach beet or swiss chard |
| **acitrón** | candied biznaga cactus |
| **adobo, adobado** | a sauce made of ground chilies, herbs and vinegar |
| **agrio** | sour |
| **agua/aguado** | water/watery |
| **agua mineral** | mineral water |
| **aguacate** | avocado |
| **aguardiente** | an alcohol made of sugar cane |
| **agujas** | ribs of beef (northern cooking) |
| **ajonjolí** | sesame |
| **albóndigas** | meat balls |
| **alcachofas** | artichokes |
| **alcaparras** | capers |
| **almejas** | clams |
| **almendras** | almonds |
| **almíbar** | light syrup |
| **almuerzo** | brunch |

73

| | |
|---|---|
| ancho | 'wide' chili |
| anguilas | eels |
| añejo | aged |
| antiguo | old, ancient |
| antojito | appetizer. Literally, 'little whim' |
| apio | celery |
| arroz | rice |
| asadero | type of cheese made in Chihuahua, Michoacán and Mexico states |
| asar/asado | grilled |
| asado al horno | broiled |
| atole | sweet gruel beverage |
| bacalao | cod fish (dried) |
| barbacoa | barbecued meat |
| berenjena | eggplant, aubergines |
| berro | watercress |
| betabel | beet |
| bizcocho | sweet buns |
| bistec | beef steak |
| birria | mutton or kid stew |
| blanco de Pátzcuaro | white fish from Pátzcuaro |
| bola/bolita | little ball |
| bolillo | bread roll |
| borracho | "drunken" i.e. including alcohol |
| botana | appetizer served with drinks |

| | |
|---|---|
| **bruselas** | brussels sprouts |
| **budín** | pudding |
| **buñuelo** | fritter |
| **burrito** | taco made with wheat flour |
| **cabrito** | kid |
| **cacahuazintle** | corn with large white kernels |
| **cajeta** | sweet goat's milk dessert |
| **calabacita** | zucchini squash |
| **calabaza** | pumpkin |
| **caldo** | broth |
| **callo de hacha** | pinna clam |
| **camarones** | shrimps |
| **camote** | yam, sweet potato |
| **cantina** | bar |
| **capeado** | covered with batter and fried |
| **capulín** | a native cherry |
| **carbón** | charcoal |
| **carne** | meat |
| **carnero** | lamb |
| **carnitas** | pieces of fried pork |
| **cascabel** | 'rattle' chili |
| **cazón** | dog fish; small shark |
| **cazuela** | earthenware casserole |
| **cebiche** | raw fish marinated in lime juice |
| **cebolla** | onion |

# Eating and Drinking

| | |
|---|---|
| cecina | thin strips of dried meat |
| cena | supper |
| cerveza | beer |
| chabacano | apricot |
| chalupa | oval tortilla filled and topped with sauce |
| chayote | vegetable pear |
| chico zapote | fruit of the chicle tree |
| chícharos | peas |
| chicharrón | crisp fried pork rind |
| chilaca | long thin dark green chili |
| chilacayote | winter squash |
| chilaquiles | dish made of stale tortillas |
| chile | chili, hot pepper |
| chilorio | cooked, shredded meat fried with paste of ground chilies and seasoning |
| chilpachole | a crab soup from Veracruz |
| chipotle | smoked chili |
| chiquihuite | basket for tortillas |
| chirimoya | cherimoya. Fruit of the custard-apple tree. |
| chocolate | chocolate |
| chongos | cooked milk curds dessert |
| chorizo | spicy pork sausage |
| chuleta | a meat chop |
| cilantro | fresh coriander |
| ciruelas | plums |

| | |
|---|---|
| ciruela pasa | prune |
| claveatado | spiked sprinkled with cloves |
| clavos | cloves |
| cocada | a coconut dessert |
| coco | coconut |
| cochinita | suckling pig |
| cocido | cooked |
| cocina | kitchen |
| colado | strained |
| col | cabbage |
| coliflor | cauliflower |
| colinabo | kohlrabi |
| comal | thin metal griddle for making tortillas |
| comida | main meal of the day |
| comino | cumin |
| copa | a drink |
| corunda | triangular tamal wrapped in corn leaves |
| crema | cream |
| crudo | raw |
| cuaresmeño | type of chili |
| cuchara | spoon |
| cuchillo | knife |
| dátiles | dates |
| desayuno | breakfast |
| deshebrar | to shred |

# Eating and Drinking

| | |
|---|---|
| dulce | sweet |
| durazno | peach |
| ejotes | green beans |
| elote | ear of fresh corn |
| enchilada | filled tortilla served in sauce |
| encurtido | pickled, preserved |
| ensalada | salad |
| envinada | wine added |
| epazote | a flavouring (herb) |
| escarola | endive |
| espárragos | asparagus |
| escabeche | pickle |
| estilo | in the style of |
| estofado | stew |
| faisán | pheasant |
| fiambre | cold cuts |
| fingido | false, ersatz |
| flameado | flambée, flaming |
| flan | caramel custard |
| flor de calabaza | pumpkin flower |
| frambuesas | raspberries |
| fresas | strawberries |
| fresco | fresh |
| frijoles | beans |
| frito | fried |
| gallina | hen |

| | |
|---|---|
| **garbanzo** | chickpea |
| **garnacha** | round appetizer of tortilla dough |
| **gordita** | thick cake of maize dough and lard |
| **granada china** | fruit. Hard orange skin, grey and white edible seeds. Similar to passion fruit |
| **granada** | pomegranate |
| **grano de elote** | corn kernel |
| **guacamole** | seasoned mashed avocado |
| **guajillo** | long, thin, dried chili |
| **guayaba** | guava |
| **guajolote** | free-range turkey |
| **guiso** | dish |
| **haba** | broad bean |
| **habanero** | chili an extremely hot |
| **harina** | flour |
| **hígado** | liver |
| **higos** | figs |
| **hongos** | mushrooms |
| **huachinango** | red snapper |
| **huauzontle** | wild green with thin, serrated leaves and spiky seeded tops (vegetable) |
| **jaiba** | small hard-shelled crab |
| **jalapeño** | small, fat green chili |

# Eating and Drinking

| | |
|---|---|
| jícama | brown, bulbous root. Sliced, used as appetizer or salad |
| jitomate | tomato |
| langosta | lobster |
| langostino | prawn |
| leche | milk |
| lechuga | lettuce |
| lenguado | flounder |
| lenteja | lentil |
| licuadora | blender |
| lima agria | a bitter lime |
| limón | lemon |
| maíz | dried corn |
| mandarina | tangerine |
| mamey | mammee |
| mango | mango |
| manzana | apple |
| masa | dough of ground dried corn and water |
| melón | cantaloupe |
| manteca | lard |
| membrillo | quince |
| menudo | a hearty tripe soup |
| mero | black grouper fish |
| metate | mortar for grinding |
| milpa | cornfield |

| | |
|---|---|
| **mochomos** | roasted or cooked meat, shredded and fried crisp |
| **mole** | potpourri. Concoction or mixture |
| **moras** | blackberries; mulberries |
| **mulato** | a type of dark black-brown chili |
| **Náhuatl** | lingua franca of peoples of central highlands. Spoken before the toltecas. Spoken today in a degenerated form. |
| **naranjo** | orange |
| **nabos** | white turnips |
| **natilla** | custard-like dessert |
| **nogada** | walnut sauce |
| **nopal** | fleshy oval pad of the Opuntia cactus |
| **nuez de Castilla** | walnut |
| **nuez** | pecan |
| **olla** | round earthenware pot |
| **ostiones** | oysters |
| **pachola** | thick, half-circle shaped piece of ground meat |
| **pagua** | a genus of avocado |
| **pámpano** | pompano. fish |
| **pan** | bread |
| **pan dulce** | sweet roll, bun |
| **pancita** | stuffed sheep's stomach |
| **papa** | potato |

| | |
|---|---|
| **papa-dzul** | Yucatecan dish of pumpkin seeds and tortillas |
| **papaya** | papaya |
| **pasas** | raisins |
| **pasilla** | dried chili chilaca |
| **pastel** | cake |
| **pato** | duck |
| **pavo** | turkey |
| **pechuga** | chicken breast |
| **pellizcada** | appetizer of tortilla dough with pinched edge, filled. |
| **pepino** | cucumber |
| **pepita** | pumpkin seed |
| **peras** | pears |
| **perón** | sour apple |
| **pescado** | fish |
| **pib, pibil** | Yucatecan pit barbecue, barbecued |
| **picado** | diced |
| **picadillo** | ground meat used as stuffing |
| **piloncillo** | brown sugar, molasses |
| **pimienta** | pepper |
| **piña** | pineapple |
| **piñones** | pine nuts |
| **pipián** | sauce of ground seeds and spices |
| **plato** | dish |
| **plátano** | banana |

| | |
|---|---|
| **plátano macho** | plantain |
| **plaza** | market or central square |
| **poblana** | large green chili |
| **pollo** | chicken |
| **postre** | dessert |
| **pozole** | soup of meat and cacahuazintle corn |
| **puchero** | stew |
| **puerco, cerdo** | pork |
| **puesto** | a stand in the market or street |
| **pulpos** | octopus |
| **pulque** | fermented sap of the agave |
| **quelite** | a wild green |
| **quemar, quemada** | to burn, burned |
| **quesadilla** | tortilla turnover |
| **queso** | cheese |
| **rábanos** | radishes |
| **raja** | strip usually of chili |
| **ranchero** | country style |
| **relleno** | stuffing |
| **res** | beef |
| **revoltijo** | rosemary greens cooked in shrimp mole, princklypears potatoes. Lenten dish. |
| **robalo** | snook |
| **sal** | salt |

| | |
|---|---|
| salchicha | sausage |
| salpicón | shedded or finely minced |
| salsa | sauce |
| salsifí | oyster plant, salsify |
| sandía | watermelon |
| sardinas | sardines |
| seco | dry |
| serrano | small, fiery green chili |
| sesos | brains |
| sierra | sawfish |
| sopa | soup |
| sopes | appetizer of tortilla dough |
| taco | tortilla wrapped around a filling (sometimes fried) and served with sauce |
| tamal | dough, or dumpling of corn beaten with lard and steamed in a corn husk or banana leaf |
| taza | cup |
| tenedor | fork |
| ternera | veal |
| tomate verde | Mexican green tomato |
| tierno | tender |
| tocino | bacon |
| toronja | grapefruit |
| torta | sandwich or roll |
| tortilla | thin, unleavened pancake of ground dried maize |

| | |
|---|---|
| **tostada** | tortilla, fried, crisp and garnished |
| **totopos** **tostaditos** | small triangular pieces of/ and crisply fried whole tortillas |
| **trigo** | wheat |
| **tuna** | prickly pear, fruit of nopal cactus |
| **uchepos** | fresh corn tamales of Michoacán |
| **uva** | grape |
| **valencia** | honeydew melon |
| **vaso** | glass |
| **verdolagas** | purslane |
| **vinagre** | vinegar |
| **xoconostle** | acidy, green prickly pear |
| **yema** | yolk |
| **yuca** | yucca |
| **zapote negro** | sapodilla or naseberry |
| **zanahoria** | carrot |
| **zarzamora** | blackberry |

# Shopping

## Buying Food

Eating out is fun but so is buying food in the many shops, markets, supermarkets and "tianguis". This latter type of market consists of make-shift stalls set up in the open air where not only fresh produce may be purchased but a wide variety of handicrafts as well, often at surprisingly low prices. As **Mexico** is a great agricultural country, many many types of foods are displayed which are unknown to the American tourist. **Mangos de Manila, chico zapote, zapote negro, mamey** are but a few of the succulent fruits available in varying seasons.

Bartering is great fun and gives the visitor the opportunity for an amicable interchange of conversation. Products usually —but not always— sell at somewhat less than the asking price.

## At the Butcher's

| | |
|---|---|
| What kind of meat is that? | ¿Qué clase de carne es esa? |
| What do you call that cut? | ¿Cómo se llama esa parte? |
| I'd like some steaks, please. | Quisiera bistecs, por favor. |
| How much does that weigh? | ¿Cuánto pesa eso? |
| Will you please trim off the fat? | ¿Puede recortar la grasa, por favor? |
| Will you take the meat off the bone? | ¿Puede quitar la carne del hueso? |
| Will you grind it? | ¿Puede molerla? |
| Please slice it very fine/thick. | Por favor, rebánela muy fina/gruesa. |

| | |
|---|---|
| Will you trim the cutlets? | ¿Puede arreglar las chuletas? |
| I'll have a little more. | Ponga un poquito más. |
| That's too much. | Eso es demasiado. |
| Put it in a plastic bag. | Póngala en una bolsa de plástico. |
| Cut it in cubes. | Córtela en tajadas. |

## VOCABULARY

| | |
|---|---|
| bacon | tocino |
| beef | carne de res |
| rib | costilla |
| rumpsteak | bistec de lomo |
| filet mignon | filete |
| roast beef | asado al horno; rosbif |
| sirloin | sirloin |
| brains | los sesos |
| cooking fat | manteca |
| cutlets/chops | chuletas |
| scallopini | el escalope |
| kidneys | los riñones |
| lamb, shoulder/leg | carnero, la espalda/la pierna |
| liver | el hígado |
| pigs' trotters | las manitas de puerco |
| pork, loin | lomo de cerdo |
| sausages | las salchichas |

## At the Fish Market

| | |
|---|---|
| Will you clean the fish? | ¿Puede limpiar el pescado? |
| Leave/take off the head/tail/fins. | Deje/quite la cabeza/la cola/las aletas. |
| Have you any shellfish? | ¿Tiene mariscos? |
| What is the name of that fish? | ¿Cómo se llama ese pescado? |

# Buying Food

## VOCABULARY

| | |
|---|---|
| anchovies | las anchoas |
| bass | la lobina |
| carp | la carpa |
| clams | las almejas |
| cod | el bacalao |
| crab | el cangrejo |
| eel | la anguila |
| herring | el arenque |
| lobster | la langosta |
| octopus | el pulpo |
| oysters | los ostiones |
| pike | el lucio |
| prawns | los langostinos |
| red snapper | huachinango |
| salmon | el salmón |
| sardines | las sardinas |
| sole | el lenguado |
| squid | los calamares |
| striped bass | robalo |
| trout | la trucha |
| tuna fish | el atún |
| white fish | blanco de Pátzcuaro |

## At the Delicatessen/Dairy

| | |
|---|---|
| What kinds of sausage do you have? | ¿Qué clases de salchicha tiene? |
| I'd like one which is mild/peppery/without garlic. | Me gustaría una dulce/una picante/sin ajo. |
| May I see your selection of patés? | ¿Puedo ver su selección de patés? |
| I prefer a coarse paté/smooth paté/game paté. | Prefiero uno basto/uno fino/uno de caza. |

| | |
|---|---|
| What is the name of that cheese? | ¿Cómo se llama ese queso? |
| Have you any goat's cheese? | ¿Tiene queso de cabra? |
| Do I have to take the whole cheese or will you cut it? | ¿Me tengo que llevar el queso entero o lo corta en trozos? |
| May I test it for ripeness? | ¿Puedo ver si está maduro? |
| Have you any bread/cookies? | ¿Tiene algo de pan/galletas dulces? |
| Do you sell breakfast cereals? | ¿Vende cereales para el desayuno? |
| I'll take a little of each salad. | Póngame un poquito de cada ensalada. |
| Have you a can of tomato puree? | ¿Tiene una lata de puré de jitomate? |
| Have you a jar of olives? | ¿Tiene un frasco de aceitunas? |

---

## VOCABULARY

| | |
|---|---|
| anchovies | las anchoas |
| garlic sausage | salchichón con ajo |
| gherkins | los pepinillos |
| ham | el jamón |
| macaroni | los macarrones |
| olives | las aceitunas |
| pickles | pepinos en escabeche |
| salami | el salami |
| salt beef | carne de res salada |
| smoked fish | el pescado ahumado |
| spaghetti | el espagueti |
| stuffed olives | las aceitunas rellenas |
| canned food | la comida en lata (latería) |

# Buying Food

## At the Grocer's/Supermarket

| | |
|---|---|
| bacon | el tocino |
| biscuits | los panecitos |
| bottle (of) | la botella (de) |
| bread | el pan |
| butter | la mantequilla |
| cereals | los cereales |
| potato chips | las papas fritas |
| dried fruit | la fruta seca |
| eggs | los huevos |
| flour | la harina |
| garlic | el ajo |
| jam | la mermelada |
| jar (of) | el frasco (de) |
| margarine | la margarina |
| oil | el aceite |
| pepper | la pimienta |
| rice | el arroz |
| salt | la sal |
| can (of) | la lata (de) |
| vinegar | el vinagre |

## At the Fruit and Vegetable Store

| | |
|---|---|
| Is the melon ripe? | ¿Está maduro el melón? |
| This lettuce is rather limp. | Esta lechuga está bastante marchita. |
| Are these fresh apples crisp? | ¿Son frescas estas manzanas? |
| How many/much will make a kilo? | ¿Cuántos(as)/cuánto harán un kilo? |
| It's for eating today/tomorrow. | Es para comer hoy/mañana. |
| Will you please weigh this bunch? | ¿Puede pesar este manojo, por favor? |

| | |
|---|---|
| Have you got a stronger bag? | ¿Tiene una bolsa más fuerte? |
| I will put it in the cart. | Lo pondré en el carrito. |
| Have you got a box? | ¿Tiene una caja? |

## VOCABULARY

| | |
|---|---|
| apples | las manzanas |
| apricots | los chabacanos |
| artichoke | la alcachofa |
| asparagus | los espárragos |
| banana | el plátano |
| beans | los frijoles |
| beets | los betabeles |
| blackberry | la zarzamora |
| broccoli | el bróculi |
| cabbage | la col |
| carrots | las zanahorias |
| cauliflower | la coliflor |
| cherries | las cerezas |
| chestnut | la castaña |
| cress | los berros |
| cucumber | el pepino |
| date | el dátil |
| fig | el higo |
| grapefruit | la toronja |
| grapes | las uvas |
| hazelnuts | las avellanas |
| leeks | los poros |
| lemons | los limones |
| lettuce | la lechuga |
| melon | el melón |
| onions | las cebollas |
| oranges | las naranjas |
| peaches | los duraznos |
| pears | las peras |

# Shopping

| | |
|---|---|
| peas | **los chícharos** |
| pineapple | **la piña** |
| plums | **las ciruelas** |
| potatoes | **las papas** |
| radishes | **los rábanos** |
| raspberries | **las frambuesas** |
| rhubarb | **el ruibarbo** |
| spinach | **la espinaca** |
| strawberries | **las fresas** |
| sweet corn (cob) | **los elotes** |
| sweet pepper | **el pimiento** |
| tangerines | **las mandarinas** |
| tomatoes | **los jitomates** |
| turnips | **los nabos** |
| green beans | **los ejotes** |

## Other Shops and Market Stalls

Shopping is fun anywhere and in Mexico there are many lovely handicrafts which are reminders of your sojourn south of the border. Hand-woven sarapes, pottery, straw baskets, copperware, are among some of the many products well worth buying.

| | |
|---|---|
| I want to go shopping. Where are the best shops? | **Quiero ir de compras. ¿Dónde están las mejores tiendas?** |
| the shops where everyone goes? | **las tiendas donde van todos?** |
| the cheaper shops? | **las tiendas más baratas?** |
| Where is the market? | **¿Dónde está el mercado?** |
| Till what time are you open? | **¿Hasta qué hora está abierto?** |
| Is there a grocer near here? | **¿Hay una tienda de comestibles cerca de aquí?** |

| | |
|---|---|
| antique shop | la tienda de antigüedades |
| art gallery | la galería de arte |
| baker | la panadería |
| bank | el banco |
| baskets | las canastas |
| beauty salon | el salón de belleza |
| blankets | los sarapes |
| bookshop | la librería |
| butcher | la carnicería |
| candy store | la dulcería |
| copperware | el artículo de cobre |
| dairy | la lechería |
| delicatessen | la salchichonería |
| department store | el almacén |
| drug store | la farmacia |
| dry cleaner | la tintorería |
| fish store | la pescadería |
| grocer | los abarrotes |
| hairdresser | el salón de belleza |
| barbershop | la peluquería |
| hardware store | la ferretería |
| jeweler's | la joyería |
| liqueur store | la tienda de licores |
| newsagent | el puesto de periódicos |
| optician | el óptico |
| photographer | el fotógrafo |
| pottery | la tienda de alfarería |
| shoemaker | el zapatero |
| shoe store | la zapatería |
| stationery store | la papelería |
| tailor | el sastre |
| toy shop | la tienda de juguetes |
| travel agent | la agencia de viajes |
| vegetable store | la verdulería |
| watchmaker | la relojería |
| wine merchant | el vinatero |

# Shopping

## Buying Clothes

| | |
|---|---|
| I'm just looking, thank you. | Estoy mirando, gracias. |
| I would like to see some shirts. | Me gustaría ver camisas. |
| plain/colored/striped. with long/short sleeves. in cotton. | sencillas/de color/rayadas. de manga larga/corta. de algodón. |
| My size is. . . | Mi talla es. . . |
| My collar size is. . . | El número de mi cuello es. . . |
| My waist/bust/hip size is. . . | Mido. . . de cintura/pecho/cadera. |
| This color does not suit me. | Este color no me va bien. |
| Have you something in wool/in red? | ¿Tiene algo en lana/en rojo? |
| It is not my style. | No es de mi estilo. |
| I want something more casual. | Quiero algo más sport. |
| Is there a fitting room where I can try it on? | ¿Hay un probador donde me lo pueda poner? |
| Can I return it if it is unsuitable? | ¿Puedo devolverlo si no me queda bien? |
| May I have a receipt? | ¿Me puede dar un recibo? |
| It does not fit. | No me sienta bien. |
| It is too large/small/tight/wide. | Es demasiado grande/pequeño/apretado/ancho. |
| Can you show me something else? | ¿Me puede enseñar otra cosa? |
| The zipper is stuck/broken. | El zipper está trabado/roto. |

## VOCABULARY

| | |
|---|---|
| camel hair | el pelo de camello |
| chiffon | la gasa |
| cotton | el algodón |
| crepe | el crepé |
| denim | el dril |
| felt | el fieltro |
| flannel | la franela |
| gabardine | la gabardina |
| lace | el encaje |
| leather | el cuero/la piel |
| linen | el lino |
| nylon | el nylón |
| pique | el piqué |
| poplin | la popelina |
| rayon | el rayón |
| satin | el raso |
| silk | la seda |
| suede | el ante |
| taffeta | el tafetán |
| tweed | el tweed |
| velvet | el terciopelo |
| wool | la lana |
| worsted | el estambre |

## MEASUREMENTS

| | |
|---|---|
| arm | el brazo |
| chest | el pecho |
| hip | la cadera |
| leg | la pierna |
| neck | el cuello |
| waist | la cintura |

## COLORS

| | |
|---|---|
| black | negro |
| blue | azul |

| | |
|---|---|
| green | **verde** |
| mauve | **malva** |
| pastel colors | **los colores pastel** |
| orange | **naranja** |
| red | **rojo** |
| rose | **rosa** |
| strong colors | **los colores fuertes** |
| violet | **violeta** |
| white | **blanca** |
| yellow | **amarillo** |

ITEMS OF CLOTHING

| | |
|---|---|
| bathing cat | **el gorro de baño** |
| bathing suit | **el traje de baño** |
| bathrobe | **la bata** |
| belt | **el cinturón** |
| blazer | **el saco sport** |
| blouse | **la blusa** |
| boots | **las botas** |
| brassiére | **el sostén** |
| buckle | **la hebilla** |
| button | **el botón** |
| cap | **la gorra** |
| coat | **el abrigo** |
| cuff links | **las mancuernillas** |
| dinner jacket | **el smoking** |
| dress | **el vestido** |
| evening dress | **el traje de noche** |
| girdle | **la faja** |
| gloves | **los guantes** |
| handkerchief | **el pañuelo** |
| hat | **el sombrero** |
| jacket | **el saco** |
| jeans | **el pantalón de mezclilla** |
| nightdress | **el camisón** |
| overcoat | **el abrigo** |
| panties | **las pantaletas** |
| pants suit | **el traje pantalón** |
| parka | **la chamarra** |

| | |
|---|---|
| pocket | el bolsillo |
| pullover | el suéter |
| pyjamas | los pijamas |
| raincoat | el impermeable |
| sandals | las sandalias |
| scarf | la mascada, la bufanda |
| shirt | la camisa |
| shoelaces | las agujetas |
| shoes | los zapatos |
| shorts | los calzones |
| skirt | la falda |
| slip | el fondo |
| slippers | las pantuflas |
| socks | los calcetines |
| stockings | las medias |
| suit | el traje |
| suspenders | los tirantes |
| t-shirt | la camiseta |
| thread | el hilo |
| tie | la corbata |
| leotards | las mallas |
| trousers | los pantalones |
| vest | el chaleco |
| zipper | el cierre |

## At the Shoe Store

| | |
|---|---|
| I want a pair of walking shoes. | Quiero un par de zapatos cómodos. |
| evening shoes | zapatos de noche. |
| moccasins. | mocasines. |
| boots | botas. |
| suede shoes | zapatos de ante. |
| slippers | pantuflas. |
| sandals | sandalias. |
| sneakers | tenis. |
| My size is. . . | Mi número es. . . |

97

## Shopping

| | |
|---|---|
| I like a wide/narrow fitting. | Quisiera de horma ancha/estrecha. |
| I want high/low heels. | Quiero tacón alto/bajo. |
| I want flat-heeled shoes. | Quiero zapatos planos |
| I want leather-soled shoes. | Quiero zapatos con suela de cuero. |
| rubber-soled shoes. | suela de goma. |
| cork-soled shoes. | suela de corcho. |
| These are not comfortable. | Estos no son cómodos. |
| May I try the other shoe? | ¿Puedo probarme el otro zapato? |
| Have you got a shoe horn? | ¿Tiene un calzador? |
| They are not my style. | No son de mi estilo. |
| What other colors do you have? | ¿Qué otros colores tiene? |
| How much are they? | ¿Cuánto valen? |
| That is more than I want to pay. | Es más de lo que quiero pagar. |
| I will wear them. Will you please wrap up my own shoes? | Los llevaré puestos. ¿Puede envolver mis otros zapatos, por favor? |
| Do you sell shoe polish/shoe cleaner/shoe brushes? | ¿Vende grasa para zapatos/limpia zapatos/cepillo para zapatos? |

## Tobacconist

| | |
|---|---|
| A pack/carton of. . . cigarettes, please. | Una cajetilla/paquete de. . . cigarros, por favor. |
| A box of matches, please. | Una caja de cerillos, por favor. |

| | |
|---|---|
| Do you sell American cigarettes? | ¿Vende cigarros americanos? |
| What is the local brand? | ¿Cuál es la marca del país? |
| Are they Virginia or French/Egyptian/Turkish/American tobacco? | ¿Son de tabaco de Virginia o francés/egipcio/turco/americano? |
| Have you any filter tips/king size/menthol? | ¿Tiene con boquilla/filtro king size/mentolados? |
| Do you sell pipe tobacco? | ¿Vende tabaco para pipa? |
| May I see your selection of pipes? | ¿Puedo ver su selección de pipas? |
| I'd like a cigar. | Quiero un puro. |
| Have you a cigar cutter? | ¿Tiene un cortador de puros? |
| Do you sell pipe cleaners? | ¿Vende escobillas? |
| I'd like some snuff. | Quiero rapé. |
| Do you have matches? | ¿Tiene cerillos? |

## VOCABULARY

| | |
|---|---|
| box | la caja |
| carton | el paquete |
| cigarette case | la cigarrera |
| cigarette lighter | el encendedor |
| flint | la piedra |
| gas | el gas |
| lighter fluid | la gasolina de encendedor |
| matches | los cerillos |
| packet | la cajetilla |
| pipe | la pipa |
| pouch | la tabaquera |

99

# Shopping

## Hardware Stores and Electrical Supply Stores

| | |
|---|---|
| I'd like a heavy-duty saucepan/a non-stick frying pan. | Quiero un cazo pesado / una sartén que no se pegue. |
| Have you a grill/charcoal? | ¿Tiene una parrilla/carbón? |
| I need a plastic/metal can for water. | Necesito un envase de plástico/metal para el agua. |
| I'll have a bucket, please. | Me da una cubeta, por favor. |
| Have you some strong twine? | ¿Tiene un mecate fuerte? |
| I need a rope and a hook. | Necesito una soga y un gancho. |
| I need a battery for my flashlight/radio. | Necesito una batería para mi linterna/radio. |

### VOCABULARY

| | |
|---|---|
| adapter | el adaptador |
| basket | el cesto/la canasta |
| battery | la batería/pila |
| brush | el cepillo |
| bulb | el foco |
| chamois leather | la gamuza |
| distilled water | el agua destilada |
| dust cloth | el trapo de sacudir |
| car radio | el radio para coche |
| fork | el tenedor |
| hammer | el martillo |
| insulating tape | la cinta aislante |
| knife | el cuchillo |
| mallet | el mazo |
| penknife | la navaja |
| percolator | la cafetera de filtro |
| plug | el enchufe |
| saw | la sierra |

100

| | |
|---|---|
| scissors | **las tijeras** |
| screwdriver | **el atornillador / desarmador** |
| razor | **la máquina de afeitar** |
| spoons | **las cucharas** |
| string | **el cordón** |
| tweezers | **las pinzas** |
| wire | **el alambre** |
| wrench | **la llave inglesa** |

## Drugstore

| | |
|---|---|
| Do I need a doctor's prescription? | **¿Necesito una receta del médico?** |
| Is there an all-night drugstore open? | **¿Hay una farmacia de guardia?** |
| Can you make up this prescription? | **¿Me puede preparar esta receta?** |
| When will it be ready? | **¿Cuándo estará lista?** |
| Will you write down the instructions in English if possible? | **¿Puede escribir las instrucciones en inglés si es posible?** |
| Is this safe/dangerous for children? | **¿Es esto seguro/peligroso para niños?** |
| Have you anything for a cold/sore throat/cough? | **¿Tiene algo para el catarro/ la garganta inflamada/ la tos?** |
| I'd like to buy a thermometer. | **Necesito un termómetro.** |
| Would you please have a look at this cut/bruise? | **Por favor, ¿puede ver esta cortada/contusión?** |
| What kind of bandage would be best? | **¿Qué clase de venda sería mejor?** |
| I've got an upset stomach. diarrhea. | **Estoy mal del estómago. diarrea.** |

**101**

| | |
|---|---|
| indigestion. | **indigestión.** |
| a headache. | **dolor de cabeza.** |
| sunburn. | **quemadura del sol.** |
| constipation. | **estreñimiento.** |

VOCABULARY

MEDICINES

| | |
|---|---|
| aspirin | **la aspirina** |
| antibiotic | **el antibiótico** |
| bandage | **la venda** |
| band-aids | **las venditas adhesivas** |
| corn plasters | **los parches para callos** |
| cough lozenges | **las pastillas para la tos** |
| cough medicine | **el jarabe para la tos** |
| cotton | **el algodón** |
| disinfectant | **el desinfectante** |
| ear drops | **las gotas para el oído** |
| gargle | **las gárgaras** |
| gauze | **la gasa** |
| insect repellent | **el repelente** |
| iodine | **el yodo** |
| iron pills | **las píldoras de hierro** |
| laxative | **el laxante** |
| lip salve | **la pomada para labios** |
| sanitary towels | **las toallas sanitarias** |
| sedative | **el calmante** |
| sleeping pill | **el somnífero** |
| thermometer | **el termómetro** |
| tranquilizers | **los sedantes** |
| vitamins | **las vitaminas** |

TOILET ARTICLES

| | |
|---|---|
| after shave lotion | **la loción para después de afeitar** |
| astringent | **el astringente** |
| bath oil | **el aceite de baño** |

| | |
|---|---|
| bath salts | las sales de baño |
| cologne | el agua de colonia |
| comb | el peine |
| cream, cleansing | la crema, limpiadora |
|   cuticle | quitacutículas |
|   foundation | de base |
|   moisturizing | hidratante |
| deodorant | el desodorante |
| emery board | la lima |
| eye pencil | el lápiz de ojos |
| eye shadow | la sombra de ojos |
| face pack | la crema para mascarilla |
| face powder | el polvo |
| hairbrush | el cepillo |
| hair spray | la laca para el pelo |
| lipstick | el lápiz labial |
| nailbrush | el cepillo de uñas |
| nail file | la lima de uñas |
| nail polish | el esmalte de uñas |
| nail polish remover | quitabarniz |
| diapers | los pañales |
| perfume | el perfume |
| plastic pants | los calzoncitos de plástico |
| rouge | el colorete |
| safety pins | los alfileres de seguridad |
| setting lotion | el fijador |
| shampoo | el champú |
| shaving cream | la crema de afeitar |
| soap | el jabón |
| suntan oil | el aceite bronceador |
| sponge | la esponja |
| talcum powder | el talco |
| tissues | los pañuelos de papel |
| toilet paper | el papel del baño |
| tooth brush | el cepillo de dientes |
| toothpaste | la pasta de dientes |

# Shopping

## At the Photographer's

| | |
|---|---|
| I'd like to buy a camera. | Quisiera comprar una cámara fotográfica. |
| One that is cheap and easy to use. | Una que sea barata y fácil de operar. |
| Will you please check my camera? | Por favor ¿puede revisar mi cámara? |
| The film gets stuck. | La película se traba. |
| The exposure meter is not working. | El exposímetro no funciona. |
| The flash does not light up. | No funciona el flash |
| The film winder is jammed. | El carrete está trabado |
| Can you do it soon? | ¿Lo puede hacer pronto? |
| Will you please develop this film? | ¿Puede revelar esta película? |
| I want some black and white/color film/color prints. | Quiero una película en blanco y negro/en color/positivas en color. |
| Is this film for use in daylight or artificial light? | Esta película se usa con la luz del día o con luz artificial? |
| I need a light meter. | Necesito un exposímetro. |
| How much is an electronic flash? | ¿Cuánto cuesta un flash electrónico? |

## VOCABULARY

| | |
|---|---|
| films 120, 127, 135, 620 | película ciento veinte/ciento veintisiete/ciento treinta y cinco/seis cientos veinte |
| 20 exposures, 36 exposures | veinte exposiciones/treinta y seis exposiciones |

104

| | |
|---|---|
| a fast film/a fine-grain film | una película rápida/de grano fino |
| movie film 8 mm/16 mm | película cinematográfica ocho milímetros/dieciséis milímetros |
| flash bulbs | los flash |
| lens | el objetivo |
| lens cap | el capuchón para el objetivo |
| red filter | el filtro rojo |
| yellow filter | el filtro amarillo |
| ultraviolet | ultravioleta |
| range finder | el telémetro |
| shutter | el obturador |
| long focus lens | el objetivo de foco largo |
| wide angle lens | el objetivo de foco ancho |
| camara case | la caja de la cámara |

## Bookshop/Stationery Store

| | |
|---|---|
| On which shelf are the books on art/history/politics/sport? | ¿En qué estante están los libros de arte/historia/política/deporte? |
| I want a pocket dictionary. | Quiero un diccionario de bolsillo. |
| Have you any American papers? | ¿Tiene periódicos norteamericanos? |
| Have you any paperbacks in English? | ¿Tiene libros de bolsillo en inglés? |
| Can you recommend an easy-to-read book in Spanish? | ¿Puede recomendarme un libro fácil de leer en español? |
| Do you sell second-hand books? | ¿Vende libros usados? |
| I want a map of the area. The scale of this one is too small. | Quiero un mapa de la zona. La escala de ésto es demasiado pequeña. |

## Shopping

| | |
|---|---|
| Have you got refills for this ballpoint pen? | ¿Tiene repuestos para esta pluma? |
| Can you please deliver the American newspaper every morning? | Por favor, ¿puede enviar el periódico americano cada mañana? |

### VOCABULARY

| | |
|---|---|
| address book | el libro de direcciones |
| box of crayons | la caja de crayones |
| carbon paper | el papel carbón |
| cellophane | el celofán |
| drawing paper | el papel de dibujo |
| envelopes | los sobres |
| note book | el cuaderno |
| fountain pen | la pluma fuente |
| greaseproof paper | el papel apergaminado |
| glue | la cola/pegamento |
| ink | la tinta |
| label | la etiqueta |
| paste | el engrudo |
| pen | la pluma |
| pencil | el lápiz/lapicero |
| pencil sharpener | el sacapuntas |
| playing cards | la baraja |
| postcards | las tarjetas postales |
| eraser | el borrador/goma |
| sellotape | la cinta adhesiva |
| silver foil | el papel estaño |
| thumb tacks | las chinches |
| tissue paper | el papel chino |
| typewriter ribbon | la cinta para máquina |
| typing paper | el papel de máquina |
| writing pad | el block de papel |

## Buying Souvenirs

| | |
|---|---|
| Are all these things made in Mexico? | ¿Todo esto es hecho en México? |
| This is a nice straw hat. | Este es un sombrero de paja bonito. |
| I like this bag. | Esta bolsa me gusta. |
| Have you any costume jewelry? | ¿Tiene joyería de fantasía? |
| I'm looking for charms for my bracelet. | Estoy buscando dijes para mi pulsera. |
| I'd like to try on that ring. | Me gustaría probarme ese anillo. |
| What is this bracelet made of? | ¿De qué está hecha esta pulsera? |
| I'd like some local pottery. | Quisiera cerámica regional. |
| Can you pack this carefully? | ¿Puede empacar esto con cuidado? |
| Do you ship things abroad? | ¿Envían cosas al extranjero? |
| I'm just looking around. | Sólo estoy mirando. |
| I'll come back later. | Volveré más tarde. |
| Can I leave a deposit on it and return tomorrow? | ¿Puedo dejar un depósito y volver mañana? |
| Do you take foreign checks? | ¿Aceptan cheques extranjeros? |

VOCABULARY

| | |
|---|---|
| beads | las cuentas |
| brooch | el broche |
| chain | la cadena |

# Shopping

| | |
|---|---|
| cigarette lighter | el encendedor |
| clock | el reloj |
| cuff links | las mancuernillas |
| earrings | los aretes |
| jewel box | el joyero |
| music box | la caja de música |
| necklace | el collar |
| ring | el anillo |
| rosary | el rosario |
| silverware | los objetos de plata |
| watch | el reloj |
| watchstrap | la correa de reloj |
| wristwatch | el reloj de pulsera |

# Entertainment

## Out for the Evening

### Nightclubs

| | |
|---|---|
| Can you recommend a nightclub with a good show? | ¿Puede recomendar un blub nocturno con un buen espectáculo? |
| a place with dancing? | un lugar para bailar? |
| a disco? | una discoteca? |
| an open-air dance floor? | una pista de baile al aire libre? |
| a nightclub with hostesses? | un cabaret con meseras? |
| Is there an entrance fee? | ¿Hay una cuota de entrada? |
| Does it include drinks? | ¿Incluye bebidas? |
| What is the cost of drinks? | ¿Cuál es el costo de las bebidas? |
| At what time does the show start? | ¿A qué hora empieza el espectáculo? |
| Is there a different price for drinks at the bar? | ¿Hay un precio diferente para las bebidas en el bar? |
| I don't want a photograph. | No quiero una foto. |
| May I have this dance? | ¿Me permite este baile? |

### Movies

| | |
|---|---|
| What's on at the movies? | ¿Qué hay en el cinema? |
| Have you got a guide to what's playing? | ¿Tiene una cartelera de espectáculos? |
| Two seats, please. | Dos asientos, por favor. |
| At what time does it start? | ¿A qué hora empieza? |

# Entertainment

| | |
|---|---|
| Will we have to wait in line for long? | ¿Tendremos que hacer fila por mucho tiempo? |
| I want a seat near the front/at the back/in the middle. | Quiero un asiento adelante/en la parte de atrás/en medio. |
| Do I tip the usherette? | ¿Le doy propina a la acomodadora? |
| I'd rather sit over there. | Preferiría sentarme por allí. |
| Will you please shine your flashlight here? | Por favor ¿puede enfocar su luz aquí? |
| I have dropped something. | Se me ha caído algo. |
| Is there an ice cream vendor? | ¿Hay un vendedor de helados? |
| At what time does the main picture start? | ¿A qué hora empieza la película principal? |
| Will you please move over to the right/left? | ¿Por favor, puede moverse hacia la derecha/izquierda? |
| Remove your hat, please. | Quítese el sombrero, por favor. |

## VOCABULARY

| | |
|---|---|
| actor | el actor |
| actress | la actriz |
| director | el director |
| dubbing | el doblaje |
| intermission | el intermedio |
| producer | el productor |
| projector | el proyector |
| screen | la pantalla |
| sound | el sonido |
| star | la estrella |

110

## Theater / Opera

| | |
|---|---|
| Is there a ticket agency here? | ¿Hay una agencia de boletos cerca? |
| Is there another way of getting a ticket? | ¿Hay otro modo de obtener un boleto? |
| Are there any last-minute returns? | ¿Hay cancelaciones de último momento? |
| Do we have to wear evening dress? | ¿Tenemos que llevar traje de noche? |
| I'd like a souvenir program. | Quisiera un programa de recuerdo. |
| What is the name of the soloist? | ¿Quién es el/la solista? |
| Who is the leading actor? | ¿Quién es el actor principal? |
| How long is the intermission? | ¿Cuánto dura el intermedio? |
| Where is the bar? | ¿Dónde está el bar? |

### VOCABULARY

| | |
|---|---|
| applause | el aplauso |
| audience | el auditorio |
| baritone | el barítono |
| bass | el bajo |
| composer | el compositor |
| conductor | el director |
| contralto | la contralto |
| encore | la repetición |
| orchestra | la orquesta |
| playwright | el dramaturgo |
| scenery | el escenario |
| soprano | la soprano |
| stage | el escenario |
| tenor | el tenor |

## Concert Hall

| | |
|---|---|
| I want a seat from which I can see the pianist's hands. | Quiero un asiento desde donde pueda observar las manos del/de la pianista. |
| Can I buy the score? | ¿Puedo comprar la música? |
| Who is conducting tonight? | ¿Quién dirige esta noche? |
| Who is the soloist? | ¿Quién es el/la solista? |

### VOCABULARY

| | |
|---|---|
| bass | el bajo |
| bassoon | el contrabajo |
| brass | los metales |
| cello | el violoncello |
| clarinet | el clarinete |
| cymbals | los platillos |
| drum | el tambor |
| flute | la flauta |
| French horn | el corno |
| percussion | los instrumentos de percusión |
| saxophone | el saxofón |
| strings | los instrumentos de cuerda |
| timpani | los tímpanos |
| trombone | el trombón |
| trumpet | la trompeta |
| violin | el violín |
| wind | los instrumentos de viento |

## Casino

| | |
|---|---|
| What games are played here? | ¿A qué se juega aquí? |
| What is the minimum stake in this room? | ¿Cuál es la mínima puesta en esta sala? |

| | |
|---|---|
| Can I buy some chips? | ¿Puedo comprar fichas? |
| I should like 5,000 pesos worth. | Quisiera el valor de cinco mil pesos. |
| Excuse me, those are my chips. | Perdone, esas son mis fichas. |
| Where can I cash my chips? | ¿Dónde puedo cobrar mis fichas? |
| I'm broke. | Estoy arruinado. |
| I'll take another card. | Deme otra carta. |
| No more. | Nada más. |
| Pass me the dice please. | Páseme los dados, por favor. |

---

## VOCABULARY

| | |
|---|---|
| ace | el as |
| bet | la apuesta |
| blackjack | veintiuno |
| cards | las cartas |
| chemin de fer | chemin de fer |
| clubs | los tréboles |
| croupier | el crupier |
| diamonds | los diamantes |
| hearts | los corazones |
| jack | la sota/la jota |
| joker | el comodín |
| king | el rey |
| poker | póker |
| queen | la reina |
| spades | las espadas |

## Out for the Day

### On the Beach

| | |
|---|---|
| Does one have to pay to use this beach? | ¿Se paga en esta playa? |
| Is there a free section of the beach? | ¿Hay un área libre en la playa? |
| Is it clean? | ¿Está limpia? |
| How much does it cost per day/per week to rent a cabin? | ¿Cuánto cuesta por día/por semana el alquiler de una cabina? |
| deckchairs? | las sillas de lona? |
| air mattress? | un colchón de aire? |
| sun umbrella? | una sombrilla? |
| Can I leave valuables in the cabin? | ¿Puedo dejar objetos de valor en la cabina? |
| Is the ticket valid all day? | ¿Sirve la entrada para todo el día? |
| Does the beach shelve steeply? | ¿Baja la playa repentinamente? |
| Is it safe for swimming? | ¿Se puede nadar sín peligro? |
| Are there any currents? | ¿Hay corrientes? |
| Is it safe to dive off the rocks? | ¿Se pueden hechar clavados desde las rocas sin peligro? |
| Where is the fresh water shower? | ¿Dónde está la regadera de agua corriente? |
| Have you any tar remover? | ¿Tiene algo para quitar el chapopote? |
| Can I rent a swimsuit? | ¿Puedo alquilar un traje de baño? |

114

I've cut my foot. Have you any bandages?

Me he cortado un pie. ¿Tiene unas vendas?

Do you keep lost property?

¿Guarda objetos perdidos?

Is there a children's beach club?

¿Hay un club de playa para niños?

At what time are the keep-fit classes?

¿A qué hora son las clases para mantenerse en forma?

Is there water-ski tuition available?

¿Hay enseñanza de esquí acuático?

Does it matter if I can't swim?

¿Importa si no sé nadar?

Where is the nearest beach shop?

¿Dónde está la tienda más cercana de la playa?

Have you got a life jacket?

¿Tiene un chaleco salvavidas?

Is this a good place for skin diving?

¿Es este un buen sitio para el buceo?

Help! I'm in difficulty!

¡Socorro! ¡Estoy en apuros!

## VOCABULARY

| | |
|---|---|
| beach ball | la pelota de playa |
| beach mattress | el colchón de aire |
| cactus | el cactus |
| goggles | las gafas submarinas |
| harpoon gun | la pistola de arpón |
| high tide | la marea alta |
| low tide | la marea baja |
| net | la red |
| pines | los pinos |
| promenade | el paseo |
| raft | la balsa |
| rocks | las rocas |

## Sightseeing

| | |
|---|---|
| row boat | la barca de remo |
| sand | la arena |
| sandals | las sandalias |
| seaweed | las algas |
| shells | las conchas |
| sun oil | el aceite para el sol |
| surf | la ola |
| surfboard | el deslizador |
| underwater | debajo del agua |
| waterski instructor | el instructor de esquí acuático |
| yacht | el yate |

## Sightseeing

| | |
|---|---|
| Where can I get a good guide book? | ¿Dónde puedo comprar una buena guía? |
| Is there an excursion around the city? | ¿Hay una excursión de la ciudad? |
| Is it a conducted tour? | ¿Es un tour con guía? |
| Am I allowed to go alone? | ¿Puedo dar una vuelta solo? |
| Where do I find an official guide? | ¿Dónde hay un guía oficial? |
| Does the whole-day excursion include lunch? | ¿Está la comida incluida en la excursión para todo el día? |
| Are the entrance fees extra? | ¿Son extra las entradas? |
| Should I tip the guide/driver? | ¿Debo dar una propina al guía/conductor? |
| I'd like to stay here longer. | Quisiera quedarme un poco más. |
| I'll meet the party later. | Me uniré más tarde al grupo. |
| Where will you be? | ¿Dónde estará? |

Will you please write it down? | ¿Lo puede escribir, por favor?

Can I hire an audioguide? | ¿Puedo alquilar un audioguía?

## In Churches

Do ladies have to cover their heads? | ¿Se deben de cubrir la cabeza las señoras?

Is it all right to enter like this? | ¿Está bien entrar así?

How old is this church? | ¿Es muy antigua esta iglesia?

Who founded it? | ¿Quién la fundó?

Are the stained glass windows original? | ¿Son estas vidrieras de colores las originales?

Can one illuminate the fresco? | ¿Se puede iluminar el fresco?

Is one allowed to go up the bell tower? | ¿Está permitido subir al campanario?

Is there a book about the church? | ¿Hay un libro acerca de la iglesia?

May I leave a small contribution? | ¿Puedo dejar una pequeña contribución?

VOCABULARY

| | |
|---|---|
| abbey | la abadía |
| aisles | los pasillos |
| altar | el altar |
| arch | el arco |
| candle | la vela |
| cathedral | la catedral |
| chapel | la capilla |
| cloister | el claustro |

# Sightseeing

| | |
|---|---|
| cross | la cruz |
| crucifix | el crucifijo |
| crypt | la cripta |
| choir | el coro |
| column | la columna |
| convent | el convento |
| fresco | el fresco |
| font | la pila |
| monastery | el monasterio |
| nave | la nave |
| sculpture | la escultura |
| shrine | el santuario |

## Art Galleries and Museums

| | |
|---|---|
| Have you a catalogue/ illustrated catalogue? | ¿Tiene un catálogo/catálogo ilustrado? |
| Are there any plaster casts? | ¿Hay vaciados? |
| Do you sell transparencies? | ¿Vende diapositivas? |
| Am I allowed to photograph? | ¿Puedo sacar fotografías? |
| May I use my tripod? | ¿Puedo usar el trípode? |
| Is the gallery open on Sundays? | ¿Está la galería abierta los domingos? |
| Is it free? | ¿Es gratis? |
| Where can I find the Modern Art School? | ¿Dónde está la escuela de Arte Moderno? |
| Do you make photocopies? | ¿Hace fotocopias? |
| Where is the library? | ¿Dónde está la biblioteca? |

VOCABULARY

| | |
|---|---|
| antique books | los libros antiguos |
| bas relief | el bajorrelieve |

118

| | |
|---|---|
| china | la porcelana |
| costumes | los vestidos |
| drawing | el dibujo |
| engraving | el grabado |
| etching | el aguafuerte |
| frame | el marco |
| furniture | los muebles |
| jewelry | las joyas |
| lithograph | la litografía |
| miniature | la miniatura |
| porcelain | la porcelana |
| pottery | la cerámica |
| silverware | la plata |

## Historical Sights

| | |
|---|---|
| Will there be far to walk? | ¿Hay que andar mucho? |
| Can I wait here till you return? | ¿Puedo esperar aquí hasta que vuelva? |
| Is there a souvenir stall? | ¿Hay un puesto de recuerdos? |
| Where can we get a cold drink? | ¿Dónde hay bebidas frescas? |
| Is there a plan of the grounds? | ¿Hay un plano de los jardines? |
| I would like to walk around the gardens. | Me gustaría pasear por los jardines. |

### VOCABULARY

| | |
|---|---|
| amphitheater | el anfiteatro |
| aqueduct | el acueducto |
| arena | la arena |
| armour | la armadura |
| battlements | el almenaje |
| cannon | el cañón |
| catacombs | las catacumbas |

119

## Sightseeing

| | |
|---|---|
| castle | el castillo |
| column | la columna |
| courtyard | el patio |
| crossbow | la ballesta |
| fort | el fuerte |
| fortifications | las fortificaciones |
| forum | el foro |
| fountain | la fuente |
| gate | la entrada |
| pediment | la cornisa de puerta |
| viaduct | el viaducto |
| wall | el muro |

## Gardens

| | |
|---|---|
| Are these gardens open to the public? | ¿Están abiertos al público los jardines? |
| Can we walk where we like? | ¿Podemos andar por donde quiera? |
| How long will it take to walk around? | ¿Cuánto se tarda en dar una vuelta? |
| At what time do you close? | ¿A qué hora cierran? |
| Is there a plan of the gardens? | ¿Hay un plano de los jardines? |
| Where is the greenhouse/ tropical plant house? | ¿Dónde está el invernadero/ el pabellón de las plantas tropicales? |
| May we sit on the grass? | ¿Nos podemos sentar en el pasto? |
| What is the name of that plant/flower? | ¿Cómo se llama esa planta/ flor? |
| Is there a lake/pond? | ¿Hay un lago/estanque? |
| Who designed these gardens? | ¿Quién planeó estos jardines? |

## VOCABULARY

| | |
|---|---|
| ash | el fresno |
| beech | la haya |
| birch | el abedul |
| bougainvillea | la buganvilia |
| carnation | el clavel |
| cherry tree | el cerezo |
| chrysanthemum | el crisantemo |
| daffodil | el narciso |
| dahlia | la dalia |
| daisy | la margarita |
| deciduos trees | los árboles de hoja caduca |
| elm | el olmo |
| evergreen | el árbol de hoja perenne |
| fir | el abeto |
| geranium | el geranio |
| herbaceous border | el borde herbáceo |
| ivy | la hiedra |
| lily | la azucena |
| moss | el musgo |
| nasturtium | la capuchina |
| oak | el roble |
| pear tree | el peral |
| pine | el pino |
| poplar | el chopo |
| rose | la rosa |
| tulip | el tulipán |
| violet | la violeta |
| wisteria | la vistaria |

## The Zoo

| | |
|---|---|
| The children would like to visit the zoo. | Los niños quisieran ver el zoológico. |
| Is it open every day? | ¿Está abierto todos los días? |
| Is there a nature reserve? | ¿Hay una reserva natural? |

# Sightseeing

| | |
|---|---|
| Can one drive through it? | ¿Se puede conducir a través? |
| Where can we park the car? | ¿Dónde podemos estacionar el coche? |
| Where can one buy animal food? | ¿Dónde se puede comprar comida para los animales? |
| When is feeding time? | ¿A qué hora se les da de comer? |
| Is there an insect house? | ¿Hay un pabellón de insectos? |
| Can the children ride an elephant? | ¿Se pueden montar los niños en el elefante? |
| Is there a children's zoo? | ¿Hay un zoológico para niños? |

## VOCABULARY

| | |
|---|---|
| antelope | el antílope |
| ants | las hormigas |
| aquarium | el acuario |
| baboon | el mandril |
| bat | el murciélago |
| bird | el pájaro |
| bison | el bisonte |
| cat | el gato |
| crocodile | el cocodrilo |
| dog | el perro |
| frog | la rana |
| giraffe | la jirafa |
| hippopotamus | el hipopótamo |
| horse | el caballo |
| hyena | la hiena |
| leopard | el leopardo |
| lion | el león |
| parrot | el loro |
| rhinoceros | el rinoceronte |
| seal | la foca |
| snake | la culebra |
| turtle | la tortuga |
| zebra | la cebra |

# Sport

Spanish-speaking people follow soccer, bicycle racing and athletics with the same enthusiasm as much of the rest of the world, but they also have sports which are uniquely their own, one of which is frontón. . . or a version of **pelota** as it is called in Spain. Two others —if they can be classified as sports— are cockfights and bullfights.

## La Corrida

The bullfight is called **la corrida**, which means, literally, running the bulls, and few people can keep calm when discussing this entertainment. In Mexico where the bullfight has a loyal following, bullfighters have the same status as film stars and are forgotten as quickly if they fail to give the public what it wants.

The bullfight is a highly formal encounter between man and beast. It begins with the running of the bull by the various **matadores**, each of whom makes the bull charge at his cape. This indicates to the matador who will have to kill it what the bull's characteristics are: whether it hooks to the right or left, turns fast, and so on.

The second stage, announced by the sounding of trumpets, introduces the **picador**, a Quixote-like figure on horseback whose role is to counter the bull's charge with a lance which damages the bull's neck muscles and therefore makes him less powerful, though not less dangerous.

The third stage is the placing of the **banderillas**, pairs of decorated barbed darts. Three pairs are placed between the bull's shoulder blades. This is accomplished by a man without a cape whose only defense against the charging beast is his own agility and speed.

# Sport

The final stage is the duel between the matador and the bull. The matador plays the bull with a smaller cape —**la muleta**— in which he carries the sword with which he will dispatch the animal. The object of this part of the **corrida** is to show the matador's skill at dominating the bull and preparing him for the moment when he will stand in the correct way so as to make the kill possible. Matadors who are trying to make their reputation, or who already have a big name to maintain, often take extraordinary risks and this provides the excitement that the crowd seeks.

The kill should be accomplished by one clean thrust, but unfortunately, this is rarely achieved. After repeated failures, the bull is dispatched by a short dagger thrust in the back of the neck. Bullfighters who have done well are rewarded by the presentation of the animal's ears, and at times, also the tail. These frequently end up in the lap of the person to whom the matador has dedicated the bull.

Bullfights start promptly at 4:30 in the afternoon when the sun is low and for this reason the best seats are those with their backs to the sun, **sombra**. These are the most expensive and the nearer they are to the arena, the steeper in price they become. **Sol y sombra** means a seat which will be in the sun for part of the **corrida** and in the shade for the latter half. A seat in the **sol** will face the sun for most of the bullfight. Bullring seats are very hard and cushions are rented out by itinerant vendors. Other vendors sell ice cream, programs and a variety of beverages.

| | |
|---|---|
| I would like to go to a bullfight. | **Quisiera ir a una corrida.** |
| Where is the bullring? | **¿Dónde está la plaza de toros?** |
| Have you got a seat in the shade/sun/open/first row? | **¿Tiene asiento de sombra/ sol/tendido/barrera?** |
| How much is it? | **¿Cuánto vale?** |

| | |
|---|---|
| Where are our seats? | ¿Dónde están nuestros asientos? |
| What is the bullfighter's name? | ¿Cómo se llama el torero? |
| Is he good? | ¿Es bueno? |
| How many bulls will he fight? | ¿Cuántos toros tiene que lidiar? |
| Can I rent a cushion? | ¿Puedo alquilar una almohadilla? |

## VOCABULARY

| | |
|---|---|
| bleachers | la grada |
| bull | el toro |
| bullfight | la corrida |
| bullfighter | el torero |
| bullfighter's costume | el traje de luces |
| bullfighter on horseback | el picador/el rejoneador |
| bullring | la plaza de toros |
| cloak | el capote |
| dart | la banderilla |
| ear | la oreja |
| hat | la montera |
| horn | el cuerno |
| legs | las patas |
| man who places the darts | el banderillero |
| ring | la arena, el ruedo |
| red cape and stick | la muleta |
| sword | la espada |
| tail | la cola |
| team | la cuadrilla |
| uncovered seats | el tendido |
| walk around the ring | la vuelta al ruedo |

# Sport

## Frontón

**Frontón** is played by two teams on a court also called **'frontón'**. Players wear a long, curved wicker basket, called the **cesta**, on their hand. The ball is hard and covered in leather. The player swings the ball along the basket and swerves it against the end wall. The ball travels very fast and it is the job of the opposing player to catch and return it.

Spectators sit along one side of the court, protected by wire, and may place bets with a bookie who shouts the odds at the crowd. Bets are placed in a most curious manner. As the spectators' seats are placed on a steep grade, bets and cash are interchanged by means of a slit in a tennis ball which is tossed between bookie and bettor.

This is an entertainment that few visitors attend, but one that should not be missed for its local color and excitement without bloodshed.

Frontón in its Spanish version is called **pelota**, literally 'ball'. In the United States it is known as 'jai-alai'.

## Football

| | |
|---|---|
| Where is the stadium? | ¿Dónde está el estadio? |
| How does one get there? | ¿Cómo se va allí? |
| Should I book tickets? | ¿Tengo que reservar entradas? |
| Will it be very crowded? | ¿Estará muy lleno? |
| Who is playing? | ¿Quiénes juegan? |
| Is there a local team? | ¿Hay un equipo local? |
| I want a ticket for the main stand/a place under cover/in the open. | Quiero un boleto de tribuna/bajo cubierta/al descubierto. |
| May I have a program? | ¿Me da un programa? |

126

VOCABULARY

| | |
|---|---|
| area | área |
| attack | el ataque |
| defense | la defensa |
| football | el futbol |
| goal keeper | el portero |
| goal posts | los postes |
| halfway line | la línea media |
| penalty area | la area de penalty |
| players | los jugadores |
| referee | el árbitro |
| scoreboard | marcador |
| team | el equipo |

## The Races

| | |
|---|---|
| I want a ticket for the paddock/a grandstand seat, please. | Quiero una entrada para el paddock/un asiento de tribuna, por favor. |
| Where can I place a bet? | ¿Dónde puedo hacer una apuesta? |
| What are the odds on number 5? | ¿Qué son los puntos de ventaja en el número cinco? |
| I'd like to back it to win/win and place/to place. | Apostaré a ganar el primer lugar/ganar y entrar/para entrar. |
| Which is the favorite? | ¿Cuál es el favorito? |
| I will back the long-shot. | Apostaré al que no es favorito. |
| Is the jockey well known? | ¿Es bien conocido el jockey? |

127

# Sport

| course | la pista |
|--------|----------|
| filly | la potranca |
| horse | el caballo |
| hurdles | las vallas/los obstáculos |
| jockey | el jockey |
| owner | el dueño |
| photo finish | el resultado comprobado por fotocontrol |
| rails | la cerca |
| stable | la cuadra |
| starting gate | la barrera de salida |
| tote (parimutuel machine) | el totalizador |
| trainer | el entrenador |

## Tennis

| Is there a tennis club nearby? | ¿Hay un club de tenis por aquí? |
|--------------------------------|----------------------------------|
| Where is the championship being held? | ¿Dónde tienen lugar los campeonatos? |
| How can I get some tickets? | ¿Cómo puedo obtener entradas? |
| Should I arrive early? | ¿Debo llegar temprano? |
| Who is playing? | ¿Quién juega? |
| Is it on hard courts or grass? | ¿Es sobre pista dura o de pasto? |
| I want to watch the men's singles/doubles/mixed doubles. | Quiero ver los juegos individuales de hombres/el juego de dobles/el juego mixto. |
| How do you score in Spanish? | ¿Cómo se puntúa en español? |

| | |
|---|---|
| 15, 30, 40, deuce, advantage in/out, game, set, match. | Quince, treinta, cuarenta, a dos, ventaja del saque/del que recibe, juego, set, partida. |
| Shall we toss for service? | ¿Echamos para el saque? |
| Let's adjust the net. | Ajustemos la red. |
| It's too high/too low. | Está demasiado alta/demasiado baja. |
| That was out/in/on the line. | Estaba fuera/dentro en la línea. |
| Good shot. | Buena tirada. |
| Will you keep the score? | ¿Puede llevar el score? |
| Change ends. | Cambien de lado. |

VOCABULARY

| | |
|---|---|
| backhand | el revés |
| forehand | el derecho |
| racket | la raqueta |
| rally | el peloteo |
| smash | el smash |
| spin | el giro de la pelota |
| tennis ball | la pelota de tenis |
| umpire | el árbitro |
| volley | la volea |

## Golf

| | |
|---|---|
| Is there a golf course nearby? | ¿Hay un campo de golf por aquí? |
| Does one have to be a member? | ¿Tiene uno que ser miembro? |
| Is there a temporary membership? | ¿Se puede ser socio temporalmente? |

# Sport

| How much does it cost to play? | ¿Cuánto cuesta jugar? |
| I'd like a caddie. | Quisiera un cadi. |
| Are there any trolleys for hire? | ¿Hay carretillas para alquilar? |
| I'd like to speak to the pro. | Quisiera hablar con el profesional. |
| Are you free for lessons? | ¿Está libre para dar clases? |
| Will you play a round with me? | ¿Quiére jugar una vuelta conmigo? |
| My handicap is eighteen. | Mi desventaja es dieciocho. |
| I can't get any length on my drive. | No puedo tirar el golpe de salida muy lejos. |
| My approach shots are weak. | Mis tiros de cerca son débiles. |
| I'll do some putting while I wait for you. | Tiraré al hoyo mientras le espero. |
| Can I hire some clubs? | ¿Puedo alquilar palos? |
| May I have a scorecard? | ¿Me da una tarjeta de tanteo? |

## VOCABULARY

| bunker | la hoya de arena |
| club house | el edificio del club |
| fairway | el recorrido |
| golf bag | el saco de golf |
| green | el césped |
| irons | el acero |
| mashie | el palo de cabeza curva |
| niblick | el palo de cabeza de hierro |
| par | el mínimo de jugadas |
| rough | el terreno quebrado |
| tee | el tee, la salida |
| to slice | cortar |

130

## Water-skiing

| | |
|---|---|
| I have never skied before. Not even on snow. | No he esquiado nunca. Ni en la nieve. |
| I am not a good swimmer. | No soy buen nadador. |
| Do I wear a life jacket? | ¿Me pongo un chaleco salvavidas? |
| Will you please help me to put on the skis? | ¿Me puede ayudar a ponerme los esquís? |
| Please pass me the rope. | Me pasa la cuerda, por favor. |
| May I ride on the speed boat? | ¿Puedo ir en la lancha? |
| Can I borrow a wetsuit? | ¿Me puede prestar un traje de hule? |
| I'm ready now. | Ya estoy listo. |
| Just a moment. | Un momento. |

VOCABULARY

| | |
|---|---|
| aquaplane | el hidroavión |
| bathing cap | el gorro de nadar |
| goggles | las gafas submarinas |
| jump | el salto |

## Riding

| | |
|---|---|
| Is there a riding stable at the resort? | ¿Hay una caballeriza con caballos para montar aquí? |
| Can I hire a horse for riding? | ¿Puedo alquilar un caballo para montar? |
| Do you give lessons? | ¿Da clases? |

**131**

# Sport

| | |
|---|---|
| I'd like to go for a ride. | Quisiera dar un paseo a caballo. |
| I want a quiet horse. | Quiero un caballo manso. |
| Have you any ponies? | ¿Tiene poneys? |
| Will an instructor accompany the ride? | ¿Habrá un instructor durante el recorrido? |
| I'd like to practice jumping. | Quisiera practicar el salto. |
| I am an experienced rider/a novice. | Soy un jinete con experiencia/un novato. |
| Do you have English saddles? | ¿Tiene albardones? |
| This horse has gone lame. | Este caballo cojea. |
| The girth is too loose. | La cincha está floja. |
| Will you please adjust my stirrups? | ¿Puede ajustar mis estribos? |
| Will you hold my horse while I mount? | ¿Puede agarrar mi caballo mientras monto? |
| Will you give me a leg-up? | ¿Me ayuda a subir? |

## VOCABULARY

| | |
|---|---|
| bit | el freno |
| blinkers | las anteojeras |
| bridle | la brida |
| girth | la cincha |
| harness | el cabestro |
| hock | el corvejón |
| hoof | el casco |
| mare | la yegua |
| martingale | la amarra |
| reins | las riendas |
| stallion | el garañón |
| withers | la cruz |

132

## Fishing

| | |
|---|---|
| Where can I get a permit to fish? | ¿Dónde puedo obtener una licencia para pescar? |
| Are there places for fishing in this area? | ¿Hay lugares para pescar en esta zona? |
| Are there any trout or salmon? | ¿Hay trucha o salmón? |
| How much does a day's fishing cost? | ¿Cuánto cuesta pescar por un día? |
| Is that per rod? | ¿Es eso por caña? |
| Where can I get some bait? | ¿Dónde puedo encontrar cebo? |
| What is the minimum size that I am allowed to keep? | ¿Cuál es el tamaño mínimo que se permite guardar? |
| What is the best time of day to go out? | ¿Cuál es la mejor hora del día para salir? |
| Are there any boats that will take me deep sea fishing? | ¿Hay alguna embarcación que me pueda llevar a la pesca de alta mar? |
| Do they provide tackle? | Proveen los aparejos? |

---

VOCABULARY

---

| | |
|---|---|
| fishing season | la temporada de pesca |
| fly | la mosca |
| float | el corcho |
| gaff | el arpón |
| hook | el anzuelo |
| line | el sedal |
| lure/bait | el cebo |
| net | la red |

## Sport

| | |
|---|---|
| reel | el carrete |
| spinner | la cuchara/el cebo |
| weights | el lastre |

## Shooting

| | |
|---|---|
| Where can I shoot? | ¿Dónde puedo cazar? |
| Do I need a license? | ¿Necesito una licencia? |
| I'd like to borrow a 12-bore shotgun. | Quisiera que me prestasen una escopeta de calibre doce. |
| I have my own rifle. | Tengo mi propio rifle. |
| Is there a shooting party I could join? | ¿Hay alguna partida de caza a la que me pueda unir? |
| Is there a clay pigeon shoot? | ¿Hay un tiro al pichón? |
| Is there a rifle range near? | ¿Hay un campo de tiro cerca? |

## VOCABULARY

| | |
|---|---|
| backsight | la mira delantera |
| barrel | el cañón |
| bullets | las balas |
| butt | la culata |
| cartridges | los cartuchos |
| catch | el pestillo |
| ejector | el expulsor |
| foresight | la mira trasera |
| hammer | el percusor |
| revolver | el revólver |
| safety catch | el seguro |
| telescopic sight | la mira telescópica |
| trigger | el gatillo |

## Sailing and Boating

| | |
|---|---|
| I'd like to hire a dinghy. | **Quisiera alquilar un bote.** |
| Is an outboard motor extra? | **¿Es un motor fuera de borda extra?** |
| Does this have an auxiliary engine? | **¿Tiene este un motor auxiliar?** |
| How many berths are there? | **¿Cuántas literas hay?** |
| How much water does it draw? | **¿Cuánto tiene de calado?** |
| Is there a stove/sink/chemical toilet? | **¿Hay un hornillo/una fregadera/un wáter químico?** |
| Are all cutlery, china and cooking utensils included? | **¿Están los cubiertos, vajilla y utensilios de cocina incluidos?** |
| Are there sheets and blankets provided? | **¿Hay provisión de sábanas y mantas?** |
| Have you got a map of the river? | **¿Tiene un mapa del río?** |
| Are there many locks to negotiate? | **¿Hay que pasar muchas esclusas?** |
| At what time do the locks close? | **¿A qué hora cierran las esclusas?** |
| How far is it to the next place where I can get fuel? | **¿Cuánta distancia hay hasta el próximo sitio donde puedo obtener combustible?** |
| Can I leave the boat here while we go to the shops? | **¿Puedo dejar aquí la lancha mientras vamos de compras?** |
| Where is the next refuse dump? | **¿Dónde está el próximo depósito de basura?** |
| Will you please give me a tow? | **¿Me puede remolcar?** |

# Sport

| anchor | el ancla |
| boat | la lancha |
| boathook | el bichero |
| bow | la proa |
| canoe | la canoa |
| chart | la carta de navegación |
| deck | la cubierta |
| diesel engine | el motor diesel |
| halyards | las drizas |
| hull | el casco |
| jib | el foque |
| keel | la quilla |
| lifebelt | el cinturón salvavidas |
| lifejacket | el chaleco salvavidas |
| mainsail | la vela mayor |
| mast | el mástil |
| motorboat | la lancha de motor |
| oar | el remo |
| paddle | el canalete |
| pennant | el gallardete |
| port (left) | el babor |
| propeller | la hélice |
| rowboat | el bote de remos |
| sail | la vela |
| sheet | la escota |
| starboard (right) | el estribor |
| steer | navegar |
| tiller | la caña del timón |
| yacht | el yate |

# Winter Sports

Winter sports simply do not exist in Mexico because of the benign climate. Although snow may be observed on the two majestic mountains —**Popocátepetl** and **Ixtaccíhuatl**—

their surfaces are rocky and therefore unsuitable for sports.
However, several Latinamerican countries —**Chile** and
**Argentina,** for example— do have winter sports. For this
reason familiarity with the relevant phraseology is useful.

| | |
|---|---|
| I'd like to join a class for beginners/intermediate skiers. | Quisiera unirme a un grupo de principiantes/esquiadores intermedios. |
| Is there a beginners' slope? | ¿Hay una ladera para principiantes? |
| Where can I hire skis? a toboggan? boots? ski sticks? | ¿Dónde puedo alquilar esquís? un tobogán? botas? bastones de esquiar? |
| I have never skied before. | No he esquiado nunca. |
| These boots are uncomfortable. | Estas botas son incómodas. |
| They are too tight/loose/big/small. | Están apretadas/anchas/grandes/pequeñas. |
| How far is the ski lift from the hotel? | ¿A qué distancia está el montacargas de esquiar del hotel? |
| Can I get a season ticket? | ¿Puedo obtener un abono? |
| Are the skiing conditions good this morning? | ¿Son buenas las condiciones de esquiar esta mañana? |
| Are all the slopes open? | ¿Están abiertas todas las pistas? |
| Is there any cross-country skiing? | ¿Hay esquí a campo traviesa? |
| Please help me. | Por favor, ¿me puede ayudar? |
| I think I've twisted my ankle. | Creo que me he torcido un tobillo. |

# Sport

| | |
|---|---|
| Two entrance tickets for the ice rink. | **Dos boletos de entrada para la pista de patinaje.** |
| Is there a heated swimming pool? | **¿Hay piscina con agua caliente?** |
| Look out! I can't stop! | **¡Cuidado! ¡No puedo parar!** |

## VOCABULARY

| | |
|---|---|
| avalanche | el alud |
| cable car | el teleférico |
| funicular | el funicular |
| ice | el hielo |
| ice skating | el patinaje sobre hielo |
| parka | una chamarra |
| skates | los patines |
| ski-lift | el teleski |
| slalom | el slalom |
| snow | la nieve |
| stem | la vuelta |
| tobaggan run | la pista de tobogán |
| waterproof pants | los pantalones impermeables |

# General Services

If you are travelling independently and have perhaps rented
an apartment or a home, phrases for dealing with gas,
electricity and plumbing problems will be indispensable.
But even when all that is taken care of by someone else,
it is useful to be able to communicate with Post Office
staff, telephone operators and other officials in their own
language.

## Post Office

| | |
|---|---|
| Where is the nearest Post Office? | ¿Dónde está el Correo más cercano? |
| What time do they open? | ¿A qué hora abren? |
| Can I cash an international money order here? | ¿Puedo cobrar aquí un giro internacional? |
| I want some stamps for a letter to the U.S.A. | Quiero estampillas para una carta a los Estados Unidos. |
| What does a post card to the United States cost? | ¿Cuál es el franqueo de una tarjeta postal a los Estados Unidos? |
| I'd like to register this letter. | Quisiera certificar esta carta. |
| I want to send it airmail express. by surface. printed matter rate. | Quiero enviarlo por avión. urgente. por correo ordinario. como impresos. |
| Where do I post parcels? | ¿Dónde puedo mandar paquetes por correo? |
| Do I need a customs form? | ¿Necesito una forma de aduana? |
| Have you a letter for me? | ¿Tiene una carta para mí? |

## General Services

| | |
|---|---|
| May I have a telegram form? | ¿Me da una forma de telegrama? |
| I'll send it by the cheap rate/air mail. | Lo enviaré por correo ordinario/por avión. |
| When will it arrive? | ¿Cuándo llegará? |
| I want to make a local telephone call. | Quiero hacer una llamada telefónica local. |
| an international call. | internacional. |
| a person-to-person call. | de persona a persona. |
| Can you reverse the charges? | ¿Puedo llamar por cobrar? |
| The line is busy. Please try again later. | El número está ocupado. Por favor, llame más tarde. |

## The Police Station

| | |
|---|---|
| I am a visitor to your country. | Estoy visitando su país. |
| I would like to report a theft/loss/accident/crime. | Quisiera reportar un robo/ una pérdida/un accidente/ un crimen. |
| Someone stole my wallet. | Alguien me ha robado la cartera. |
| Something was stolen from my car/hotel room. | Han robado de mi coche/ de mi habitación del hotel. |
| The theft occurred on Juarez Avenue at about four o'clock. | El robo ocurrió en la Avenida Juárez a eso de las cuatro de la tarde. |
| I have lost my watch on the beach. | He perdido mi reloj en la playa. |
| It is valuable. | Es de valor. |
| it has sentimental value. | Tiene valor sentimental. |

140

| | |
|---|---|
| I will offer a reward. | Ofreceré recompensa. |
| Someone has been knocked down. | Alguien ha sido atropellado. |
| A lady has broken her leg. | Una señora se ha roto la pierna. |
| There is a man bothering women on the promenade. | Hay un hombre molestando mujeres por el paseo. |
| I have been swindled. | Me han estafado. |
| Can a police officer come with me? | ¿Puede venir un policía conmigo? |
| I will be a witness. | Haré de testigo. |
| I cannot be a witness. | No puedo hacer de testigo. |
| I didn't see what was happening. | No vi lo que ocurrió. |
| Is there anyone who speaks English? | ¿Hay alguien que hable inglés? |

## Electricity

| | |
|---|---|
| The lights have gone out. | Se han apagado las luces. |
| The power plug is not working. | El enchufe eléctrico no funciona. |
| The fuse has gone. | El fusible se ha fundido. |
| I think it's the switch. | Creo que es el apagador. |
| There is a smell of burning. | Huele a quemado. |
| The stove won't light. | La estufa no se prende. |
| The heating has broken down. | La calefacción no funciona. |
| Can you repair it right away? | ¿Puede arreglarla inmediatamente? |

# General Services

| | |
|---|---|
| Where is the fuse box? | ¿Dónde está la caja de fusibles? |
| Which is the main switch? | ¿Cuál es el interruptor principal? |

## VOCABULARY

| | |
|---|---|
| adaptor | el adaptador |
| bulb | el foco |
| electric fire | el fuego eléctrico |
| extension wire | el cable de extensión |
| fuse wire | el alambre del fusible |
| hairdryer | el secador de pelo |
| insulating tape | la cinta aislante |
| iron | la plancha |
| kitchen | la cocina |
| plug | el enchufe |
| radio | la radio |
| razor plug | el enchufe para la rasuradora |
| refrigerator | el refrigerador |
| spotlight | el spot |
| television | la televisión |
| flashlight | la linterna |
| water heater | el calentador de agua |

## Gas

| | |
|---|---|
| There is a smell of gas. | Huele a gas. |
| It must be a gas leak. | Debe de ser una fuga de gas. |
| The gas jet won't light. | El gas no prende. |
| The pilot light keeps going out. | La luz piloto se apaga. |
| Is there any danger of an explosion? | ¿Hay peligro de una explosión? |

142

| | |
|---|---|
| I think the ventilator is blocked. | Creo que el ventilador está obstruído. |
| We can't get any hot water. | No sale el agua caliente. |

VOCABULARY

| | |
|---|---|
| chimney, fireplace | la chimenea |
| gas stove | la estufa de gas |
| gas light | la luz de gas |
| gas main | la cañería maestra de gas, el alimentador |
| gas pipe | el tubo del gas |
| gas tap | la llave del gas |
| boiler | el calentador de agua |
| hammer | el martillo |
| key | la llave |
| monkey wrench | la llave inglesa |
| spanner | la llave de tuercas |
| water heater | el calentador de agua |

## Plumbing

| | |
|---|---|
| Are you the plumber? | ¿Es usted el plomero? |
| The sink/drain is clogged up. | El fregadero/desague está tapado. |
| There is a blockage in the pipe. | La cañería está bloqueada. |
| The faucet is dripping | La llave gotea. |
| The faucet needs a new washer. | La llave necesita un empaque nuevo. |
| This water pipe is leaking. | Hay una fuga en este tubo. |
| The toilet cistern won't fill. | El depósito del baño no se llena. |
| The valve is stuck. | La válvula no se mueve. |

143

## General Services

| | |
|---|---|
| The float is punctured. | **El flotador está picado.** |
| The water tank has run dry. | **El tanque de agua está seco.** |
| The tank is overflowing. | **El tanque está rebosando.** |

### VOCABULARY

| | |
|---|---|
| basin | **el lavabo** |
| bath | **el baño** |
| immersion heater | **el calentador de inmersión** |
| main drainage | **el alcantarillado** |
| water mains | **la cañería principal** |
| drainage | **la cañería de desague.** |
| plug | **el tapón** |
| stopcock | **la llave de cierre** |

# Personal Services

This section suggests useful phrases for such occasions as a visit to a doctor, dentist, hairdresser, hospital or barbershop.

## At the Doctor's

| | |
|---|---|
| Can you recommend a doctor? | ¿Me puede recomendar un médico? |
| Is there an English-speaking doctor in the resort? | ¿Hay un médico que hable inglés en el lugar? |
| Where is the doctor's office? | ¿Dónde está el consultorio? |
| I have an appointment. | Tengo una cita. |
| My name is. . . | Mi nombre es. . . |
| Can the doctor come to the hotel/house? | ¿Puede el médico venir al hotel/a la casa? |
| I'm not feeling well. | No me siento bien. |
| I feel sick/dizzy/faint/shivery. | Me encuentro enfermo/mareado/débil/con escalofríos. |
| The pain is here. | Tengo el dolor aquí. |
| I have a fever. | Tengo fiebre. |
|     headache. |     dolor de cabeza. |
|     back ache. |     dolor de espalda. |
|     sore throat. |     dolor de garganta. |
|     sunburn. |     quemadura de sol. |
| I have been like this since yesterday. | He estado así desde ayer. |
| I have been vomiting. | He tenido vómito. |
| I have diarrhea. | Tengo diarrea. |
| I am constipated. | Estoy estreñido. |

**145**

| I have hurt my. . . | He lastimado mi. . . |
| Do you want me to take my clothes off? | ¿Quiére que me quite la ropa? |
| Is it serious? | ¿Es grave? |
| Should I stay in bed? | ¿Debo de guardar cama? |
| Should I arrange to go home? | ¿Debo de irme a mi país? |
| I am allergic to. . . | Tengo alergia a. . . |
| I have a heart condition. | Sufro del corazón. |
| I am asthmatic/diabetic. | Tengo asma/diabetes. |
| Do I have to pay for hospitalization and medicines? | ¿Tengo que pagar por hospitalización y medicinas? |
| It's only a slight problem. | Es sólo un ligero problema. |

## VOCABULARY

### PARTS OF THE BODY

| ankle | el tobillo |
| appendix | el apéndice |
| arm | el brazo |
| artery | la arteria |
| back | la espalda |
| bladder | la vejiga |
| blood | la sangre |
| bone | el hueso |
| bowels | los intestinos |
| breast | el seno |
| cheek | la mejilla |
| chest | el pecho |
| chin | la barbilla |
| collar bone | la clavícula |

|  |  |
|---------|---------|
| ear | el oído |
| elbow | el codo |
| eye | el ojo |
| face | la cara |
| fingers | los dedos |
| foot | el pie |
| forehead | la frente |
| gland | la glándula |
| hand | la mano |
| heart | el corazón |
| heel | el talón |
| hip | la cadera |
| intestine | el intestino |
| jaw | la mandíbula |
| joint | la articulación |
| kidney | el riñón |
| knee | la rodilla |
| leg | la pierna |
| lip | el labio |
| liver | el hígado |
| lung | el pulmón |
| mouth | la boca |
| muscle | el músculo |
| neck | el cuello |
| nerve | el nervio |
| nose | la nariz |
| penis | el pene |
| rib | la costilla |
| shoulder | el hombro |
| skin | la piel |
| spine | la espina |
| stomach | el estómago |
| tendon | el tendón |
| thigh | el muslo |
| throat | la garganta |
| thumb | el pulgar |
| toe | el dedo (del pie) |
| tongue | la lengua |
| tonsils | las amígdalas |

|  |  |
|---|---|
| urine | la orina |
| vein | la vena |
| vagina | la vagina |
| womb | la matriz |
| wrist | la muñeca |

## INDISPOSITIONS

|  |  |
|---|---|
| abscess | el absceso |
| asthma | el asma |
| bite (dog/insect) | la mordedura/picadura |
| blisters | las ampollas |
| boil | el furúnculo |
| burn/scald | la quemadura |
| chill | el resfriado |
| cold | el catarro |
| convulsions | las convulsiones |
| cramp | el calambre |
| cut | la cortada |
| diabetes | la diabetes |
| diarrhea | la diarrea |
| dizziness | el mareo |
| hemorrhoids | las hemorroides |
| hay fever | la fiebre del heno |
| indigestion | la indigestión |
| infection | la infección |
| inflammation | la inflamación |
| influenza | la gripe |
| irritation | la irritación |
| nausea | la náusea |
| piles | las almorranas |
| rash | la urticaria |
| rheumatism | el reumatismo |
| scald | la quemadura |
| shivers | el escalofrío |
| stiff neck | la tortícolis |
| sunstroke | la insolación |
| tonsilitis | la amigdalitis |
| ulcer | la úlcera |

| | |
|---|---|
| whooping cough | la tosferina |
| wound | la herida |

## At the Dentist's

| | |
|---|---|
| I need an appointment as soon as possible. | Necesito una cita tan pronto como sea posible. |
| I have a toothache/an abscess. | Tengo un dolor de muelas/un abceso. |
| Can you suggest a painkiller until I can see you? | ¿Puede sugerir algo para el dolor hasta que le vea a Usted? |
| The bad tooth is at the front/back/side. | El diente que me duele está en el frente/atrás/a un lado. |
| Can you extract it? | ¿Lo puede sacar? |
| Does it need a filling? | ¿Necesita una tapadura? |
| Can you put in a temporary filling? | ¿Lo puede tapar provisionalmente? |
| Can I bite normally? | ¿Puedo morder como siempre? |
| I'd prefer gas to an injection. | Prefiero gas a una inyección. |
| My gums are bleeding. | Me sangran las encías. |
| I have broken my dentures. | He roto mis dentaduras. |
| What is your fee? | ¿Cuánto son sus honorarios? |

## At the Optician's

| | |
|---|---|
| I have broken my glasses. | He roto mis anteojos. |
| Can you repair them temporarily? | ¿Los puede arreglar provisionalmente? |

## Personal Services

| | |
|---|---|
| The lens is broken. Can you get a new one quickly? | **He roto la lente. ¿Puede reemplazarla pronto?** |
| Have you got contact lenses? | **¿Tiene lentes de contacto?** |
| I'd like a pair of dark glasses. | **Quisiera un par de anteojos oscuros.** |
| Do you sell binoculars/a magnifying glass/sunglasses? | **¿Tiene binoculares/una lupa/anteojos oscuros?** |
| I had better have an eye examination. | **Será mejor que me gradúe la vista.** |
| I am shortsighted/longsighted. | **Soy miope/présbita.** |
| How long will it take to make some new glasses? | **¿Cuánto tardará para hacerme unas gafas nuevas?** |
| How much will they cost? | **¿Cuánto van a costar?** |

## At the Chiropodist's

| | |
|---|---|
| I have a painful corn. | **Me duele un callo.** |
| Can you remove it? | **¿Me lo puede quitar?** |
| My bunion is rubbing against my shoe. | **El zapato me roza el juanete.** |
| I have a hard spot on the ball of my foot. | **Tengo un punto duro en la bola del pie.** |
| My nails need attention. One of them is ingrowing. | **Necesito que me atienda las uñas. Tengo un uñero.** |
| Have you anything to soften them? | **¿Tiene algo para ablandarlas?** |
| The soles of my feet are very sore. | **Tengo muy adoloridas las plantas de los pies.** |

## At the Hairdresser's or Beauty Parlor

Where is the nearest hairdresser? is there one in the hotel?

¿Dónde está el peluquero más cercano? ¿Hay uno en el hotel?

I'd like to make an appointment.

¿Me puede dar una cita?

I want it cut and shaped.

Lo quiero cortado y con forma.

shampooed and set.

lavado y prendido.

I wear it brushed forward with bangs.

Lo uso peinado hacia delante y con un flequito.

I like it brushed back.

Me gusta peinado hacia atrás.

Can you put some waves/ curls in it?

¿Me puede poner ondas/ hacer rizos?

Draw it back into a bun.

Recójalo atrás en un chongo.

I'd like the ends bleached.

Me gustarían las puntas aclaradas.

Can you give me a color rinse?

¿Me puede dar reflejos?

I think I will have it dyed.

Creo que me lo teñiré.

Have you got a color chart?

¿Tiene una muestra de colores?

No hairspray, thank you.

Nada de spray, gracias.

I'd like a manicure.

Quisiera una manicura.

What is the name of this nail polish?

¿Cómo se llama este barniz?

I'd like a complete beauty treatment, please.

Quisiera un tratamiento de belleza, por favor.

**151**

# Personal Services

| | |
|---|---|
| auburn | **castaño** |
| blond | **rubio** |
| brunette | **moreno** |
| brush | **el cepillo** |
| comb | **el peine** |
| to comb | **peinar** |
| drier | **el secador** |
| hairnet | **la redecilla** |
| hairpiece | **el pelo postizo** |
| hair pin | **la horquilla** |
| razor | **la navaja** |
| red | **pelirrojo** |
| rollers | **los rollos** |
| scissors | **las tijeras** |
| shampoo | **el champú** |
| styling | **el estilo** |
| wig | **la peluca** |

# At the Beauty Salon

I'd like a complete beauty treatment, please.

Quisiera un tratamiento de belleza, por favor.

    just a facial.
    to change my make-up.
    something more suitable for the seaside.
    something lighter in tone.
    a more open-air look.

    solo un masaje facial.
    cambiar mi maquillaje.
    algo más conveniente para la playa.
    algo mas ligero de tono.
    un aspecto más ligero.

Can you please suggest a new eye make-up?

¿Me puede sugerir un maquillaje nuevo para los ojos?

I have a delicate skin.

Tengo la piel delicada.

I think is too heavy.

**Me parece demasiado fuerte.**

Have you any false eyelashes?

**¿Tiene pestañas postizas?**

Perhaps my eyebrows need plucking.

**Quizás mis cejas necesitan depilación.**

I'd like to see some new lipstick colours.

**Quisiera ver colores nuevos de lápiz labial.**

## At the Laundry / Cleaner's

I'd like them washed / cleaned and pressed, please.

**Los quiero lavados / limpios y planchados, por favor.**

Will this stain come out? It is coffee / blood / grease / biro.

**¿Se quitará esta mancha? Es café / sangre / grasa / pluma**

Will you iron the shirts?

**¿Puede planchar las camisas?**

I will collect them tomorrow.

**Las recogeré mañana.**

Do you deliver?

**¿Hacen entrega?**

Do you do mending?

**¿Hacen zurcidos ?**

This tear needs patching.

**Este rasgón necesita un zurcido**

Can you sew this button on?

**¿Puede coser este botón?**

Can you mend this invisibly?

**¿Puede hacer en esto un zurcido invisible?**

This blouse / coat / dress is not mine.

**Esta blusa / abrigo / vestido no es mía / mío.**

My trousers are missing.

**Faltan mis pantalones.**

This was not torn when I brought it to you.

**Esto no estaba rasgado cuando se lo traje.**

# Personal Services

| How long does the launderette stay open? | ¿Hasta cuándo está abierta la lavandería automática? |
|---|---|

## VOCABULARY

| | |
|---|---|
| bleach | la lejía/blanqueador |
| cleaning fluid | el quitamanchas |
| clothes hanger | el gancho |
| cold/hot/warm water | el agua fría/caliente/templada |
| launderette | la lavandería automática |
| to press | planchar |
| rinse | aclarar |
| soap powder | el jabón en polvo |
| spin dry | secar con centrífuga |
| tumble dry | secar completamente |
| (the) washing | el lavado |
| washing machine | la máquina de lavar |

# At the Men's Hairdresser's

| I want a haircut, please. | Quiero un corte de pelo, por favor. |
|---|---|
| Just a trim. I haven't much time. | Sólo recortar las puntas. No tengo mucho tiempo. |
| Please give me a shampoo. | Un lavado de cabeza, por favor. |
| I would like it cut shorter. | Me gustaría más corto. |
| Leave it long. | Déjelo largo. |
| You are taking too much off. | Me está cortando mucho. |
| Take a little more off the back/sides/top. | Quite un poco más por atrás/ por los lados/por arriba. |
| I part my hair the left/right. | Me hago la raya en la izquierda/derecha. |

154

| | |
|---|---|
| I'd like an alcohol rub/ a singe. | Quisiera un masaje fricción de alcohol/un quemado de puntas. |
| Please give me a shave. | Aféiteme por favor. |
| Please trim my beard/ moustache/sideboards. | Recórteme la barba/el bigote/las patillas, por favor. |
| No thank you, I do not want a facial massage. | No gracias, no quiero un masaje facial. |
| I will have a manicure. | Quiero que me haga la manicura. |
| May I have a hand towel? | ¿Me puede dar una toalla de las manos? |
| Put some eau de cologne on but no cream. | Deme agua de colonia, pero no crema. |
| Move the mirror a bit more to the right. | Mueva el espejo un poco más a la derecha. |
| Yes, that's fine. | Sí, así está bien. |

# Making Friends

| | |
|---|---|
| Good morning/good afternoon/good evening. | **Buenos días/buenas tardes/ buenas noches.** |
| May I introduce myself? | **Permítame que me presente.** |
| my friend John? | **le presento a mi amigo Juan.** |
| my wife? | **le presento a mi esposa.** |
| I am. . . | **Me llamo. . .** |
| How do you do? | **Tanto gusto en conocerle.** |
| Are you staying at this hotel/this resort? | **¿Reside en este hotel/este lugar?** |
| Are you enjoying your holiday? | **¿Está pasando bien las vacaciones?** |
| How long have you been on holiday? | **¿Cuánto tiempo hace que está de vacaciones?** |
| Do you always come here? | **¿Viene siempre aquí?** |
| I'd like you to meet my friend. | **Quisiera presentarle a mi amigo.** |
| Would you care to have a drink with us? | **¿Quiére tomar una copa con nosotros?** |
| What would you like? | **¿Qué quiere?** |
| Please. I insist that you let me pay. | **Por favor. Insisto en que me deje pagar.** |
| I'm afraid that I don't speak Spanish very well. | **Lo siento pero no hablo muy bien el español.** |
| It is very nice to talk with Mexicans. | **Es muy agradable hablar con mexicanos.** |

| | |
|---|---|
| What part of Mexico do you come from? | ¿De qué parte de México es? |
| I am here with my wife/ husband/family/friends. | Estoy aquí con mi esposa/ marido/familia/mis amigos. |
| Are you alone? | ¿Está usted solo? |
| We come from Princeton, New Jersey. | Somos de Princeton, Nueva Jersey. |
| Have you been to the United States? | ¿Ha estado en los Estados Unidos? |
| If you come, please let me know. | Me comunica si viene. |
| This is my address. | Esta es mi dirección. |
| I hope to see you again soon. | Espero verle pronto. |
| Perhaps you would like to meet for a drink after dinner? | Quizás nos podamos ver para tomar una copa después de la cena. |
| I would be delighted to join you. | Con mucho gusto. |
| At what time shall I come? | ¿A qué hora vengo? |
| Have you got a family? | ¿Tiene familia? |
| Would you like to see some photos of our house/our children? | ¿Quiére ver unas fotos de nuestra casa/nuestros hijos? |
| Are you going to the party? | ¿Va a la fiesta? |
| Would you like to join our group? | ¿Le gustaría unirse a nuestro grupo? |
| I has been very nice to meet you. | Estoy encantado de conocerle. |
| You have been very kind. | Es usted muy amable. |

# Making Friends

## Dating Someone

| | |
|---|---|
| Are you on vacation? | ¿Está de vacaciones? |
| Do you live here? | ¿Vive aquí? |
| Do you like this place? | ¿Le gusta este lugar? |
| I've just arrived. | Acabo de llegar. |
| What is there to do? | ¿Qué se puede hacer? |
| I don't know anyone here. | No conozco aquí a nadie. |
| I'm with a lot of students. | Estoy con un grupo de estudiantes. |
| I'm travelling alone. | Estoy viajando solo. |
| I'm on my way around America. | Estoy viajando por toda América. |
| I come from New York/Canada/London/Australia. | Soy de Nueva York/Canadá/Londres/Australia. |
| Do you mind if I try my Spanish on you? | ¿Le importa si practico mi español con usted? |
| My Spanish is not very good. | Mi español no es muy bueno. |
| Would you like a drink? | ¿Quiére tomar algo? |
| What are you doing this evening? | ¿Qué hace esta noche? |
| Would you like to go to a discotheque? | ¿Le gustaría ir a una discoteca? |
| join our party? | unirse a nuestro grupo |
| Do you like dancing/concerts/the opera? | ¿Le gusta bailar/los conciertos/la ópera? |
| Can I walk along with you? | ¿Puedo acompañarle? |
| Which way are you going? | ¿Por dónde va? |
| Do you mind if I sit here? | ¿Le importa que me siente aquí? |

| | |
|---|---|
| This is my friend, Tom. | Este es mi amigo, Tomás. |
| Do you have a girl friend? | ¿Tiene novia? |
| We could make a foursome. | Podríamos hacer un grupo de cuatro. |
| Do you play tennis/golf? | ¿Juega al tenis/golf? |
| Do you go swimming? | ¿Usted nada? |
| Which beach do you go to? | ¿A qué playa va? |
| Would you like to come for a drive/boat ride? | ¿Le gustaría dar una vuelta en coche/en lancha? |
| It would be nice if you would. | Será estupendo si viene. |
| Thanks for coming out with me. | Gracias por salir conmigo. |
| I enjoyed it. | Lo he pasado bien. |
| Can we meet again? | ¿Le puedo ver de nuevo? |
| How about tomorrow? | ¿Mañana? |
| No thanks, I'm busy. | No, gracias, estoy ocupado(a). |
| Please stop bothering me. | Deje de molestarme. |

## Mutual Interest

| | |
|---|---|
| Do you play cards? | ¿Juega a las cartas? |
| Would you like to make a foursome at bridge? | ¿Le gustaría completar un cuarto de bridge? |
| We play canasta/poker/rummy. | Jugamos a la canasta/al póker/al rummy. |
| It is an English game. | Es un juego inglés. |
| Are you a chess player? | ¿Es jugador de ajedrez? |
| I'll ask the manager if the hotel has a chess board. | Le preguntaré al gerente si hay un tablero de ajedrez en el hotel. |

## Making Friends

| | |
|---|---|
| This is your king/queen/ knight/bishop/castle/pawn. | Este es su rey/reina/caballo/ alfil/torre/peón. |
| We could play checkers or dominoes. | Podíamos jugar a las damas o al dominó. |
| There is a ping pong table in the hotel. Would you care for a game? | Hay una mesa de ping pong en el hotel. ¿Le gustaría jugar una partida? |
| Do you read English? | ¿Puede leer inglés? |
| Would you like to borrow this book/newspaper? | ¿Le puedo prestar este libro/periódico? |

In Mexico, one may encounter a "Spanish" deck of playing cards. It consists of four suits: **copas** shown as a drinking goblet; **bastos** as a wooden club; **espadas** as swords and **oros** as gold pieces. The suits are numbered from one to seven and the court cards are page, knight (instead of queen) and king (**sota/caballo/rey**).

---

# Conversations

There are certain universal subjects of conversation which provide a bridge for communication with strangers all over the world. Among these are the weather, families, home, the cost of living and pets. The following conversational phrases are designed to start you off on an acquaintanceship with people who do not speak English.

## About the Weather

| | |
|---|---|
| It's a fine day. | Hace un día bueno. |
| It's not a very nice day. | No es un día muy bueno. |
| Will it rain all day/later/ tomorrow, do you think? | ¿Cree que lloverá todo el día/ más tarde/mañana? |

160

| | |
|---|---|
| It's going to be hot/cold today. | Va a hacer calor/frío hoy. |
| It's rather windy. | Hace bastante viento. |
| I think there is a thunderstorm coming. | Creo que se aproxima una tormenta. |
| Look at the lightning. | Mire los relámpagos. |
| It will soon clear up. | Se pasará pronto. |
| We don't get this kind of weather at home. | No tenemos esta clase de tiempo en mi país. |
| It's a pity it is so cloudy. | Es una pena que esté tan nublado. |
| Did you see the beautiful sunrise/sunset? | ¿Vio la salida de sol/puesta de sol tan bonita? |
| We had a very good/very poor summer last year. | Tuvimos un verano muy bueno/muy malo el año pasado. |
| There's a lot of haze today. | Hay mucha neblina hoy. |
| The atmosphere is very clear. | La atmósfera está muy despejada. |
| Is it cold here in the winter? | ¿Hace frío aquí en el invierno? |
| I love the spring/summer/autumn. | Me gusta la primavera/el verano/el otoño. |
| What does the barometer say? | ¿Qué marca el barómetro? |

---

VOCABULARY

| | |
|---|---|
| breeze | la brisa |
| cloudburst | el chaparrón |
| cloudy | nublado |
| drizzle | la llovizna |
| dry | seco |

# Making Friends

| forecast | el pronóstico |
| hail | el granizo |
| meteorological office | la oficina meteorológica |
| mist | la niebla |
| office | la oficina |
| pressure | la presión |
| raining | lloviendo |
| sleet | el aguanieve |
| snow | la nieve |
| sunny | soleado |
| temperature | la temperatura |
| weather report | el boletín meteorológico |
| wet | húmedo |

# About Families

| This is my wife/husband/daughter/son. | Esta(e) es mi esposa/marido/hija/hijo. |
| My son is an architect/doctor/student/teacher/engineer. | Mi hijo es arquitecto/médico/estudiante/maestro/ingeniero. |
| My daughter is at school. | Mi hija va al colegio. |
| She is taking her examinations. Then she will go to the university/art school/teacher's training college. | Tiene exámenes. Después irá a la universidad/a la escuela de arte/la normal de maestros. |
| She learned some Spanish at school. | Aprendió algo de español en el colegio. |
| My wife is Scottish, but her mother is Spanish. | Mi esposa es escocesa, pero su madre es española. |
| My father was a teacher. | Mi padre fue profesor. |
| The children prefer to take their vacation on their own. | Los hijos prefieren ir de vacaciones solos. |

162

| | |
|---|---|
| They prefer camping. | **Prefieren ir de camping.** |
| My eldest/youngest son/ daughter is married and lives in. . . | **Mi hijo/hija mayor/menor está casado(a) y vive en. . .** |
| Would you like to see some photos of our family? | **¿Quiére ver unas fotos de nuestra familia?** |
| The younger children stayed at home with their grandparents. | **Los hijos más pequeños se quedaron en casa con los abuelos.** |
| Are these your children? | **¿Son éstos sus hijos?** |
| The boy/girl looks like his/her mother/father. | **El niño/la niña se parece a su madre/padre.** |
| How old is he/she? | **¿Cuántos años tiene?** |
| My daugher is fourteen. | **Mi hija tiene catorce años.** |

---

VOCABULARY

| | |
|---|---|
| aunt | **la tía** |
| birthday | **el cumpleaños** |
| cousin | **el primo/la prima** |
| divorce | **el divorcio** |
| in-law | **(pariente) político** |
| marriage | **el matrimonio** |
| relatives | **los parientes** |
| uncle | **el tío** |
| wedding | **la boda** |

## About Homes

| | |
|---|---|
| We have a house in town/in the country. | **Tenemos una casa en la ciudad/en el campo.** |
| It is a one-family two-story house. | **Es una casa independiente de dos pisos.** |

**163**

| | |
|---|---|
| a cottage. | un chalet. |
| a small house. | una casita. |
| an apartment. | un piso. |

We have a large garden/a patio.

Tenemos un jardín grande/un patio.

There are two living rooms. One has a French window and the other a bay window.

Hay dos estancias. Una tiene una puerta ventana y la otra un mirador.

There is a fireplace in the dining room.

Hay una chimenea en el comedor.

The whole house is centrally heated/air conditioned.

Toda la casa tiene calefacción central/aire acondicionado.

We have two garages.

Tenemos dos garages.

The back garden has a lawn and swimming pool.

El jardín de atrás tiene césped y una alberca.

In our village there are many old houses.

En nuestro pueblo hay muchas casas viejas.

We prefer a modern/old house.

Preferimos una casa moderna/vieja.

What kind of house do you have?

¿Qué clase de casa tiene?

I like colonial style houses.

Me gustan las casas de estilo colonial.

Do you cook by gas or electricity?

¿Cocinan con gas o electricidad?

In a warm climate stone floors are delightful.

Los pisos de baldosas son estupendos en un clima templado.

Wall to wall carpeting makes a house warm in winter.

Alfombras de muro-a-muro hacen la casa caliente en el invierno.

Built-in cupboards make a room seem larger.

Los armarios empotrados hacen parecer una habitación más grande.

Old furniture is lovely but very expensive.

Los muebles antiguos son muy bonitos pero muy caros.

## VOCABULARY

| | |
|---|---|
| balcony | el balcón |
| brick | el ladrillo |
| ceiling | el techo |
| chimney, fireplace | la chimenea |
| door | la puerta |
| drains | los desagues |
| foundations | los cimientos |
| gable | el gablete |
| mains (electricity) | el alimentador eléctrico |
| plumbing | las cañerías |
| roof | el tejado |
| stone | la piedra |
| stone floors | las baldosas |
| terrace | la terraza |
| thatch | la paja |
| wall | la pared |
| water mains | cañería principal |
| window | la ventana |
| window frame | el marco de la ventana |
| window pane | el vidrio |
| wood | la madera |

## On Business

I have an appointment with the manager.

Tengo una cita con el director.

I am from Smith and Company.

Soy de Smith y Compañía.

# On Business

| | |
|---|---|
| Here is my card. | Aquí está mi tarjeta. |
| It is good of you to see me. | Es muy amable en recibirme. |
| May I show you our catalogue/samples? | ¿Puedo enseñarle nuestro catálogo/nuestras muestras? |
| My company manufactures knitwear. | Mi compañía confecciona ropa en tejido de punto. |
| We are looking for agents. | Buscamos representantes. |
| Our wholesale prices/retail prices are on this list. | Nuestros precios de venta al mayoreo/menudeo están en esta lista. |
| There is a special discount for a large quantity. | Hay un descuento especial por grandes cantidades. |
| Delivery is within four weeks/six months/immediate. | La entrega será dentro de cuatro semanas/seis meses/inmediata. |
| The prices are F.O.B. | Los precios son libre a bordo. |
| I would like to see your products. | Quisiera ver sus productos. |
| Have you a showroom in the town? | ¿Tiene una sala de exposición en la ciudad? |
| What are your terms of business? | ¿Cuál es su plazo de negocios? |
| Do you already have agents in my country? | ¿Tiene ya representantes en mi país? |
| Can you make modifications on this model? | ¿Puede hacer modificaciones en este modelo? |
| May I take some samples with me? | ¿Puedo llevarme unas muestras? |
| I will give you an order now. | Le haré un pedido ahora. |
| Can you look after the packing and shipping? | ¿Puede ocuparse del embalaje y transporte en barco? |

There is only a small
market for these goods.

**Hay un mercado muy
pequeño para estos productos.**

---

VOCABULARY

| | |
|---|---|
| balance sheet | el balance |
| banker | el banquero |
| bill | la factura |
| bill of exchange | la letra de cambio |
| certificate | el certificado |
| clerk | el empleado |
| contract | el contrato |
| correspondence | la correspondencia |
| credit | el crédito |
| debit | el débito / carga |
| draft | el giro / la letra de cambio |
| export | la exportación |
| freight | el flete |
| import | la importación |
| insurance | el seguro |
| invoice | la factura |
| merchant | el comerciante |
| receipt | el recibo |
| remittance | el envío |
| sale | la venta |
| warehouse | el almacén |

# Looking After Your Money

## The Bank

| | |
|---|---|
| Where is the nearest bank? | ¿Dónde está el banco más cercano? |
| Do you accept travellers' checks at this bank? | ¿Aceptan cheques de viajero en este banco? |
| Do you issue cash against a credit card? | ¿Puede darme dinero en efectivo con una tarjeta de crédito? |
| I am expecting a remittance. | Espero un giro. |
| I have a letter of credit. | Tengo una carta de crédito |
| I would like a draft to send off. | Quisiera una letra de cambio para mandar fuera. |
| What is the rate of exchange for the pound/dollar/Canadian dollar? | ¿A cómo está el cambio de la libra/el dólar/el dólar canadiense? |
| What is your commission charge? | ¿Cuánto cargan de comisión? |
| I will have it all in 100 peso bills. | Démelo todo en billetes de cien pesos. |
| Please give me 50 pesos worth of change. | Deme cincuenta pesos en cambio, por favor. |
| Can you split this check into several currencies? | ¿Puede pagarme este cheque en diversas monedas extranjeras? |
| I'll have dollars. | Deme dólares. |
| Can I open a temporary bank account? | ¿Puedo abrir una cuenta provisional? |

| | |
|---|---|
| Can you arrange for some money to be sent from my bank in New York? | ¿Puede arreglar que transfieran dinero de mi banco en Nueva York? |
| I seem to be ten pesos short. Can you please count it again? | Me parece que me ha dado diez pesos de menos. ¿Lo puede contar de nuevo? |
| Have you a card showing current exchange rates? | ¿Tiene una lista al corriente con los tipos de cambio? |

## VOCABULARY

| | |
|---|---|
| Bank of Manhattan | el Banco de Manhattan |
| cashier | el cajero |
| check book | el talonario de cheques |
| coins | las monedas |
| credit | el crédito |
| debit | el debe |
| deposit slip | la ficha de depósito |
| foreign exchange regulations | las regulaciones de divisas |
| manager | el director |
| bills | los billetes |
| signature | la firma |
| treasury | hacienda |

| | |
|---|---|
| COINS | 5 centavos |
| | 10 centavos |
| | 20 centavos |
| | 50 centavos |
| | 1 peso |
| | 5 pesos |
| | 10 pesos |

| | |
|---|---|
| BILLS | 10 pesos (minted both in coins and bills) |
| | 20 pesos |
| | 50 pesos |
| | 100 pesos |

# Money Matters

500 pesos
1000 pesos
5000 pesos
10000 pesos

## Money Exchange Offices

Are you open outside banking hours?

¿Está abierto fuera de las horas bancarias?

Does the rate of exchange alter outside normal hours?

¿Altera el índice de cambio fuera de las horas normales?

Are you open on Sundays?

¿Abren los domingos?

Can you show me your rates of exchange?

¿Me puede enseñar los índices de cambio?

Do you give the same rate for bills as for travellers' checks?

¿Paga la misma cantidad por billetes que por cheques de viajero?

## On Losing Travellers' Checks or Credit Cards

When this happens you should immediately notify the company that has issued the checks or card but you may need help from a local hotel manager or banker.

I have lost my travellers' checks/credit card.

He perdido mis cheques de viajero/mi tarjeta de crédito.

May I ask them to communicate with me through you?

¿Puedo decirles que se comuniquen conmigo por medio de ustedes?

Have you an American representative?

¿Tienen un representante americano?

I hope they will be able to refund the cheques quickly. I have no other money.

Espero que me puedan reembolsar los cheques rápidamente. No tengo otro dinero.

170

I will ask my bank at home to send you some money.

Will you accept an American check in payment of the hotel bill?

Pediré a mi banco que les envíen dinero.

¿Pueden aceptar un cheque americano como pago de la cuenta del hotel?

# Reference Section

## Numbers

| | |
|---|---|
| 1 | uno |
| 2 | dos |
| 3 | tres |
| 4 | cuatro |
| 5 | cinco |
| 6 | seis |
| 7 | siete |
| 8 | ocho |
| 9 | nueve |
| 10 | diez |
| 11 | once |
| 12 | doce |
| 13 | trece |
| 14 | catorce |
| 15 | quince |
| 16 | dieciséis |
| 17 | diecisiete |
| 18 | dieciocho |
| 19 | diecinueve |
| 20 | veinte |
| 21 | veintiuno |
| 22 | veintidós |
| 23 | veintitrés |
| 24 | veinticuatro |
| 25 | veinticinco |
| 26 | veintiséis |
| 27 | veintisiete |
| 28 | veintiocho |
| 29 | veintinueve |
| 30 | treinta |
| 31 | treinta y uno |
| 32 | treinta y dos |
| 33 | treinta y tres |

| | |
|---|---|
| 34 | treinta y cuatro |
| 35 | treinta y cinco |
| 36 | treinta y seis |
| 37 | treinta y siete |
| 40 | cuarenta |
| 50 | cincuenta |
| 60 | sesenta |
| 70 | setenta |
| 80 | ochenta |
| 90 | noventa |
| 100 | cien |
| 101 | ciento uno |
| 110 | ciento diez |
| 200 | doscientos |
| 1000 | mil |
| 1001 | mil uno |
| 1100 | mil cien |
| 2000 | dos mil |
| 1,000,000 | un millón |
| 1,000,000,000 | mil millones |

| | |
|---|---|
| first | primero |
| second | segundo |
| third | tercero |
| fourth | cuarto |
| fifth | quinto |
| sixth | sexto |
| seventh | séptimo |
| eighth | octavo |
| ninth | noveno |
| tenth | décimo |

| | |
|---|---|
| once | una vez |
| twice | dos veces |
| three times | tres veces |
| half | medio |
| quarter | cuarto |
| third | tercio |
| eighth | octavo |

# Reference Section

| | |
|---|---|
| a pair of | un par de |
| a dozen | una docena |
| a gross | una gruesa |

## Phrases Referring to Numbers

| | |
|---|---|
| Two heads are better than one. | Dos cabezas piensan mejor que una. |
| Two and two make four. | Dos y dos son cuatro. |
| The last shall be first. | Los últimos serán los primeros. |

# Time

| Greenwich Mean time | horario de Greenwich |
| Central European time | horario centroeuropeo |
| Atlantic time | horario atlántico |
| Date line | línea de cambio de fecha |
| A.M./P.M. | antes/después del medio día |
| 24 hour clock | reloj de veinticuatro horas |
| summer time | horario de verano |
| it is 12:15 | son las doce y cuarto |
| it is 12:20 | son las doce y veinte |
| it is 12:30 | son las doce y media |
| it is 12:35 | veinticinco para la una |
| it is 12:45 | cuarto para la una |
| it is 1:00 | es la una |
| midnight | medianoche |
| midday | mediodía |

## Phrases Referring to Time

| What time is it? | ¿Que hora es? |
| It is late. | Es tarde. |
| It is early. | Es temprano. |
| Are we on time? | ¿Estamos a tiempo? |
| At what time shall we meet? | ¿A qué hora nos encontramos? |
| At what time are we expected? | ¿A qué hora nos esperan? |
| On the hour. | A la hora en punto. |
| Day by day. | Día tras día. |
| By the minute. | Por minuto. |
| Every second. | Cada segundo. |
| At regular intervals. | A intervalos regulares. |

| After the clock strikes. | Después que el reloj dé la hora. |
| Days, weeks and years. | Días, semanas y años. |
| Sunday. | domingo. |
| Monday. | lunes. |
| Tuesday. | martes. |
| Wednesday. | miércoles. |
| Thursday. | jueves. |
| Friday. | viernes. |
| Saturday. | sábado. |
| daybreak. | amanecer. |
| dawn | amanecer. |
| morning | mañana. |
| afternoon. | tarde |
| evening | tarde |
| night. | noche |
| today. | hoy. |
| yesterday. | ayer. |
| tomorrow. | mañana. |
| the day before yesterday. | antes de ayer. |
| two days ago. | hace dos días. |
| the day after tomorrow. | pasado mañana. |
| the following day. | el día siguiente. |
| weekday. | día laborable. |
| a day off | día libre. |
| birthday. | cumpleaños. |
| Christmas Day. | Navidad. |
| New Year's Day | Año Nuevo |
| All Saints' Day | Todos los Santos |
| May Day | primero de mayo |
| weekend | fin de semana |
| last week | la semana pasada |
| next week | la semana próxima |
| for two weeks | por dos semanas |
| January | enero |
| February | febrero |
| March | marzo |
| April | abril |
| May | mayo |
| June | junio |

| | |
|---|---|
| July | julio |
| August | agosto |
| September | septiembre |
| October | octubre |
| November | noviembre |
| December | diciembre |
| calendar month | mes |
| lunar month | mes lunar |
| monthly | mensualmente |
| since January | desde enero |
| last month | el mes pasado |
| next month | el mes próximo |
| the month before | el mes anterior |
| the first of the month | el primero de mes |
| the first of March | el primero de marzo |
| spring | primavera |
| summer | verano |
| autumn | otoño |
| winter | invierno |
| years | años |
| B.C. | antes de Jesucristo |
| A.D. | después de Jesucristo |
| leap year | año bisiesto |

## Temperature Equivalents

| FAHRENHEIT | | CELSIUS (Centigrade) |
|---|---|---|
| 212 | Boiling point | 100 |
| 100 | | 37.8 |
| 98.4 | Body temperature | 37 |
| 86 | | 30 |
| 77 | | 25 |
| 68 | | 20 |
| 50 | | 10 |
| 32 | Freezing point | 0 |
| 0 | | 18 |

To convert Fahrenheit to Celsius, subtract 32 and divide by 1.8. To convert Celsius to Fahrenheit, multiply by 1.8 and add 32.

## Pressure

The barometer tells you the air pressure of the atmosphere. 15 lbs. per sq. in. is normal air pressure at sea level. This equals 1.1 kg. per sq. cm.

A tire gauge tells you the pressure of your car tires.

| POUNDS PER SQUARE INCH | KILOGRAMS PER SQUARE CENTIMETER |
|---|---|
| 16 | 1.12 |
| 18 | 1.17 |
| 20 | 1.41 |
| 22 | 1.55 |
| 24 | 1.69 |
| 26 | 1.83 |
| 28 | 1.97 |

## Measurements of Distance

One kilometer = 1000 meters = 0.62 miles
One hundred centimeters = 1 meter = 3.3 feet
One centimeter = 0.39 inches

The following tables give equivalents for meters and feet.
The figure in the center column can stand for either feet or
meters and the equivalent should then be read off in the
appropriate column.

| METERS | METERS AND FEET | FEET |
|--------|-----------------|------|
| 0.30 | 1 | 3.28 |
| 0.61 | 2 | 6.56 |
| 0.91 | 3 | 9.84 |
| 1.12 | 4 | 13.12 |
| 1.52 | 5 | 16.40 |
| 1.83 | 6 | 19.68 |
| 2.13 | 7 | 22.97 |
| 2.44 | 8 | 26.25 |
| 2.74 | 9 | 29.53 |
| 3.05 | 10 | 32.81 |
| 3.35 | 11 | 36.09 |
| 3.66 | 12 | 39.37 |
| 3.96 | 13 | 42.65 |
| 4.27 | 14 | 45.93 |
| 4.57 | 15 | 49.21 |
| 4.88 | 16 | 52.49 |
| 5.18 | 17 | 55.77 |
| 5.49 | 18 | 59.05 |
| 5.79 | 19 | 62.34 |
| 6.10 | 20 | 65.62 |
| 7.62 | 25 | 82.02 |
| 15.24 | 50 | 164.04 |
| 22.86 | 75 | 246.06 |
| 30.48 | 100 | 328.08 |

# Reference Section

| MILES | MILES AND KILOMETERS | KILOMETERS |
|-------|----------------------|------------|
| 0.62  | 1   | 1.61   |
| 1.24  | 2   | 3.22   |
| 1.86  | 3   | 4.82   |
| 2.49  | 4   | 6.44   |
| 3.11  | 5   | 8.05   |
| 3.73  | 6   | 9.66   |
| 4.35  | 7   | 11.27  |
| 4.97  | 8   | 12.88  |
| 5.59  | 9   | 14.48  |
| 6.21  | 10  | 16.09  |
| 15.53 | 25  | 40.23  |
| 31.07 | 50  | 80.47  |
| 46.60 | 75  | 120.70 |
| 62.14 | 100 | 160.93 |

For motorists it is useful to remember that:

30 miles = 48.3 km.

70 miles = 112.7 km.

70 km. = 43.75 miles

100 km. = 62.50 miles

To convert kilometers to miles, divide by 8 and multiply by 5.

To convert miles to kilometers, divide by 5 and multiply by 8.

# MEASUREMENTS OF QUANTITY

## Weight

| POUNDS | POUNDS AND KILOGRAMS | KILOGRAMS |
|--------|----------------------|-----------|
| 2.20 | 1 | 0.45 |
| 4.40 | 2 | 0.90 |
| 6.61 | 3 | 1.36 |
| 8.82 | 4 | 1.81 |
| 11.02 | 5 | 2.27 |
| 13.23 | 6 | 2.72 |
| 15.43 | 7 | 3.18 |
| 17.64 | 8 | 3.63 |

| OUNCES | GRAMS |
|--------|-------|
| 0.5 | 14.12 |
| 1 | 28.35 |
| 2 | 56.70 |
| 3 | 85.05 |
| 4 | 113.40 |
| 5 | 141.75 |
| 6 | 270.10 |
| 7 | 198.45 |
| 8 (1/2 lb.) | 226.80 |
| 12 | 340.19 |
| 16 (1 lb.) | 453.59 |

One kilogram = 1000 grams = 2.2 lbs.

Half a kilogram = 500 grams = 1.1 lb.

When shopping for small items, Latinamericans usually order by the 100 grams; this is about 3 1/2 ounces.

One metric ton = 1000 kilograms.

# Reference Section

## Liquid Measures

| AMERICAN PINTS | AMERICAN PINTS AND LITERS | LITERS |
|---|---|---|
| 2.19 | 1 | 0.46 |
| 4.38 | 2 (one quart) | 0.92 |
| 6.57 | 3 | 1.38 |
| 8.76 | 4 | 1.84 |
| 10.95 | 5 | 2.30 |
| 13.14 | 6 | 2.76 |
| 15.33 | 7 | 3.22 |
| 17.52 | 8 (one gallon) | 3.68 |
| 19.71 | 9 | 4.14 |
| 21.90 | 10 | 4.60 |

1 liter = 2.19 pints

One tenth of a liter = 1 deciliter = .22 of a pint

One hundredth of a liter = 1 centiliter or .022 of a pint

One hundred liters = 1 hectoliter or 27.33 gallons

One gallon = 3.68 liters

One quart = 1.38 liters

One pint = 0.46 liter

# CLOTHING SIZES

Measurements for clothes are measured according to the metric system. Here are the sizes for the main articles of clothing.

## Women

### DRESSES AND SUITS

| | | | | | | | |
|---|---|---|---|---|---|---|---|
| American | 32 | 34 | 36 | 38 | 40 | 42 | 44 |
| European | 40 | 42 | 44 | 46 | 48 | 50 | 52 |

## Men

### SUITS

| | | | | | | |
|---|---|---|---|---|---|---|
| American and Mexican | 36 | 38 | 40 | 42 | 44 | 46 |
| European | 46 | 48 | 50 | 52 | 54 | 56 |

### SHIRTS

| | | | | | | | |
|---|---|---|---|---|---|---|---|
| American and Mexican | 14 | 14 1/2 | 15 | 15 1/2 | 16 | 16 1/2 | 17 |
| European | 36 | 37 | 38 | 39 | 41 | 42 | 43 |

### SHOES

| | | | | | | | |
|---|---|---|---|---|---|---|---|
| American and Mexican | 2 | 3 | 4 | 5 | 6 | 7 | 8 | 9 |
| European | 32 | 33 | 34 | 35 | 36 | 37 | 38 | 39 |

# Index

**184**